BUTS
OF THE
BIBLE

Biblical Characters and the Crossroads of Life

Booklet 1

Genesis -
Deuteronomy

BCF

BUTS OF THE BIBLE
BIBLICAL CHARACTERS AND THE CROSSROADS OF LIFE
BOOKLET 1

This study booklet for the *Buts of the Bible* small-group study is published by the Biblical Counseling Foundation, Inc. (BCF), a non-profit, non-stock corporation founded in 1974 and incorporated in the Commonwealth of Virginia, USA, in 1977. A *Leader's Guide* is also available as a companion to this study booklet.

Scripture taken from the New American Standard Bible, © 1960, 1962, 1963, 1968, 1971, 1972, 1973, 1975, 1977 by The Lockman Foundation. Used by permission.

ISBN 978-1-60536-081-2

First Printing, December 2019

Biblical Counseling Foundation
42550 Aegean St.
Indio, CA 92203 USA

760.347.4608 telephone
760.775.5751 fax

orders@bcfministries.org email for material orders

admin@bcfministries.org email for other communications

877.933.9333 (in USA) for orders only

For information about other materials available through BCF, please visit: www.bcfministries.org

content	*page*
INTRODUCTION	**VII**
LESSON 1 **"BUT GOD, BEING RICH IN MERCY"** Where It All Starts (from Ephesians 2:4)	**1**
LESSON 2 **"BUT FROM THE TREE OF THE KNOWLEDGE OF GOOD AND EVIL"** Dealing with Temptation (from Genesis 2:17)	**9**
LESSON 3 **"BUT FOR CAIN AND HIS OFFERING"** A Lesson on False Spirituality (from Genesis 4:5)	**17**
LESSON 4 **"BUT NOAH FOUND FAVOR"** Living Righteously When It's Not Popular (from Genesis 6:8)	**27**
LESSON 5 **"BUT THROUGH THE RIGHTEOUSNESS OF FAITH"** When Our Faith is Tested Like Abraham's (from Romans 4:13)	**35**
LESSON 6 **"YET THE CHIEF CUPBEARER DID NOT REMEMBER JOSEPH"** A Lesson on Unfairness (from Genesis 40:23)	**45**
LESSON 7 **"BUT GOD MEANT IT FOR GOOD"** A Lesson on Forgiveness (from Genesis 50:20)	**53**
LESSON 8 **"BUT MOSES SAID TO GOD, 'WHO AM I?'"** How God Gets Our Attention (from Exodus 3:11)	**61**
LESSON 9 **"NEVERTHELESS THE PEOPLE WHO LIVE IN THE LAND ARE STRONG"** A Lesson on Conquering Fear (from Numbers 13:28)	**71**

The *Leader's Guide* for Booklet 1 is available as a free download from the BCF website

INTRODUCTION

OVERVIEW OF THE *BUTS OF THE BIBLE* SERIES

Welcome to the *Buts of the Bible* small-group study, published by the Biblical Counseling Foundation. BCF has been producing biblically-based discipleship and counseling materials and training since 1974. Like BCF's other materials, the *Buts of the Bible* study is designed to provide churches and individuals with in-depth life-application of God's Word.

Buts of the Bible is BCF's first series of character studies. Here we focus on individuals from both the Old and New Testaments, looking at their circumstances, struggles, temptations, spiritual defeats, and victories. This study does not examine every detail about a biblical character. Instead, the emphasis is on major events, decisions, or crossroads in their lives. From this, we will draw practical application for our own lives.

Whether they are regarded as spiritual giants or lesser-known figures, these biblical characters were still human and remarkably similar to us. We are separated by thousands of years, and the context of their situations may be different. Yet we share the same struggles and temptations, and face similar decisions. That's what makes this study so powerful. The biblical lessons they learned (or didn't learn) are relevant and applicable to our lives today.

There are three studies in this series: two sets of "buts" for the Old Testament and one set of "buts" for the New Testament. Each booklet contains nine lessons designed to span nine weeks. However, some lessons have additional material, so you can go longer if you choose.

The lessons are a fill-in-the-blank format, with descriptive background information, Scriptures to look up, and questions to answer. While this study was designed for small groups like home Bible studies, Sunday School classes, or discipleship groups, you can easily go through it on your own as well.

WHY IS IT CALLED *BUTS OF THE BIBLE?*

When we read through an account in the Bible, we can often overlook a small word like "but." However, in many cases, this little word can be an indication that something big is happening. For the biblical characters we will study, the word translated "but" (or similar phrase) often marks a turning point or a choice the character made. This word can be revealing in our own lives as well. Let's look at a few examples of how we use the word "but" today. We might use it:

- As a statement of resolve ("Charlie lost a leg, but he never complained.")
- To express a choice ("I know I would save money if I didn't report my tips, but I have to be honest.")
- To justify our behavior ("But Johnny did it to me first.")
- To procrastinate ("It's getting late, but I can play one more game before I start studying.")
- To make excuses ("I know it was due, but you didn't give me enough time!")
- As a warning ("This pill will help you, but only take one a day")

The word "but" helps us to see change of direction or contrast in circumstance, in character, or in action. To illustrate, let's look at one contrast in *Ephesians 2.*

> *"And you were dead in your trespasses and sins" (verse 1) "… But God, being rich in mercy, because of His great love with which He loved us, even when we were dead in our transgressions, made us alive together with Christ …" (verses 4-5)*

The "but" in *verse 4* highlights the stark contrast between our helpless state and God's character of love and mercy. We will observe many more of these types of "buts" in this series, and you will be amazed at how much we can learn in looking at these pivotal moments. How did the biblical characters respond to what God commanded? What does this show us about God Himself and our relationship with Him today? What set these characters apart from the people around them? The answers to these questions will supply practical applications for the situations we face in our own lives.

Note on translation of the word "but": In the Old Testament, the Hebrew language did not use a specific word for "but." However, the idea is conveyed and translated for us in English (or whichever language you are using). In the New Testament, the Greek words *alla* and *de* are often translated "but," though other versions might translate them as "nevertheless," "however," "on the contrary," "rather," "yet," "now," or "and." No matter how it is translated, the contrast is still conveyed. It is the idea the "but" represents that we will focus on. The dilemmas encountered and the choices these biblical characters made can be understood in the same way.

May God use His timeless Word to help you walk more closely with Him.

LESSON 1

"BUT GOD, BEING RICH IN MERCY"
- WHERE IT ALL STARTS -
(FROM EPHESIANS 2:4)

Before we give some background on the *Buts of the Bible* study, take a few minutes to ponder the following question:

In what ways do you think people today are similar to or different from the way they were in biblical times? Your answers can cover a range of topics, but make sure you include differences or similarities in attitudes and actions. Your group may also discuss the reasons for your answers.

HOW DO YOU THINK THEY ARE SIMILAR?	HOW DO YOU THINK THEY ARE DIFFERENT?
1.	

We will address this question a little later in this lesson.

ABOUT THE *BUTS OF THE BIBLE* SERIES

The *Buts of the Bible* series is a small-group or personal study of both Old and New Testament characters. Each lesson will focus on one character (or group of characters). Rather than looking at their entire story, this study focuses on particular events or crossroads in their lives. We will look at their examples with a view toward practical application to our lives today.

BUT GOD, BEING RICH IN MERCY

The study is in workbook format with Scripture passages to read and questions to answer. These will lead you through the biblical characters' circumstances and will challenge you to think about similar decisions or situations in your life. If you are new to studying the Bible, your group leader and fellow participants will help you. The questions are easy to answer, so don't be intimidated.

If you are studying as a group, normally you will go through each lesson together, taking turns reading Scripture passages and answering questions. As an option, you can study the lessons individually before gathering, and focus on the highlights when you meet as a group. The lessons are designed to be a little over an hour long, but could last longer, depending on how much discussion you have.

Following Lesson 1, the first Old Testament booklet contains the following lessons:

- Lesson 2 — "But from the Tree of the Knowledge of Good and Evil" — Dealing with Temptation (from Genesis 2:17)
- Lesson 3 — "But for Cain and His Offering" — A Lesson on False Spirituality (from Genesis 4:5)
- Lesson 4 — "But Noah Found Favor" — Living Righteously When It's Not Popular (from Genesis 6:8)
- Lesson 5 — "But through the Righteousness of Faith" — When Our Faith is Tested Like Abraham's (from Romans 4:13)
- Lesson 6 — "Yet the Chief Cupbearer Did Not Remember Joseph" — A Lesson on Unfairness (from Genesis 40:23)
- Lesson 7 — "But God Meant It for Good" — A Lesson on Forgiveness (from Genesis 50:20)
- Lesson 8 — "But Moses Said to God, 'Who Am I?'" — How God Gets Our Attention (from Exodus 3:11)
- Lesson 9 — "Nevertheless the People Who Live in the Land Are Strong" — A Lesson on Conquering Fear (from Numbers 13:28)

INTRODUCTION

But

Just read through any book or magazine, and you will find liberal use of that potent little word. We use the word "but" throughout our daily conversations and usually don't even think about it. Yet that little word speaks volumes. It reveals a great deal about our view of the world, our view of God, of others, and of ourselves.

BUT GOD, BEING RICH IN MERCY

Think of different ways we use the word "but." Write down at least two example statements and describe how the word "but" is used. Your group leader will ask for volunteers to share their examples.

2. _____

_____

_____

_____

"But" also serves as a descriptive word in the Bible, as it can reveal a pivotal moment. There is a great deal we can learn from both Old Testament and New Testament characters when we look at these points in their lives. They may not have used the same wording, but the idea is conveyed to us from the original languages to show:

- A contrast in attitude or action,
- Choices that biblical characters faced,
- The resolve they had in difficult situations, and
- Excuses that they sometimes gave.

We will observe biblical characters as they struggled with whether to choose a godly path, as they sought to overcome difficult circumstances, and as they interacted with others. When we look at the contrasts and pivotal points in their lives, we will see that *they were very much like us.* Their situations and responses will teach us about the decisions we face in our own lives and how we can apply God's word within those situations.

This is why there is great value in biblical character studies. *Romans 15:4* sums this up very succinctly: *"For whatever was written in earlier times was written for our instruction, so that through perseverance and the encouragement of the Scriptures we might have hope."* We trust that you will truly be encouraged and see the hope that these biblical lessons from earlier times can bring. So let's get started.

MAN'S CHARACTER AND GOD'S WISDOM

Let's go back to that first question about similarities and differences between biblical times and today. Certainly, there are cultural differences. We have also seen dramatic advances in transportation, communications, agriculture, medicine, technology, and many other aspects of life. But God's Word shows us that people's struggles, weaknesses, and responses to the situations of life have not changed. This is true regardless of culture, historical timing, age or gender. The circumstances and situations might look a little different, but the human heart is remarkably still the same.

For example, read the passages listed below. As you read, identify the characteristics (attitudes and behaviors) that are similar to what we see today. The first one is done for you, but you should look it up so you can understand the situation.

BUT GOD, BEING RICH IN MERCY

BIBLICAL SITUATION	ATTITUDE OR BEHAVIOR EXHIBITED IN THE SITUATION
3. Joshua 7:1	Greed, stealing, deceit
Numbers 14:1-4	
2 Samuel 11:2-4	
James 2:2-4	

All of these are the same things we deal with today. Pride, selfishness, lust, hate, fear, anger, murder, and many other sins and temptations have been with us from the beginning. None of them is a surprise to God. Just as He knew the biblical characters we will study, He knows our hearts and He knows exactly what we struggle with (for additional background on this, read *1 Samuel 16:7, Psalm 139:23, Jeremiah 11:20,* and *Romans 8:27* on your own). In fact, since He is our Creator, He knows us even better than we know ourselves.

Read *Hebrews 4:12-13*. What does this tell you about God and His Word?

4. _____

_____

_____

Many people might think that having nothing hidden from God's sight is a scary thing, and it can be. But why should this also give a believer hope?

5. _____

_____

_____

Because God made us and knows everything about us — our character, our hearts, our thoughts — this gives us all the more reason to seek His wisdom and insight. This study is not about our own opinions or collective human wisdom, but rather about what we can learn from God Himself, as He has revealed through the Scriptures. What does God say in *Isaiah 55:8-11* about God's thoughts, His ways, and His Word?

6. His thoughts: _____

His ways: _____

His Word: _____

_____

BUT GOD, BEING RICH IN MERCY

Everything God wants us to know about living is recorded in the Bible. God's Word is the most powerful source of wisdom available to us; so in seeking answers to the questions of life, we must always ask, "What does God say about that?"

THE MOST FUNDAMENTAL "BUT" OF ALL

Before we look at biblical characters starting in Lesson 2, let's first cover the most important "but" in our spiritual lives. It has to do with our relationship with the Lord, as this relationship is foundational and necessary before we put anything else into practice.

God wants to have a loving father/child relationship with each of us. However there is a problem. Every single one of us has gone our own way. Our sin separates us from Him. But God gives us hope — a way to restore that relationship. Let's look at a couple of verses that illustrate this further. Turn to *Romans 6:23*. What does the first part of the verse tell you?

7. _____

_____

_____

Think about the word "wages." What picture is it giving here?

8. _____

_____

_____

In the next phrase we see one of the great "buts" of the Bible, contrasting death with eternal life. What else does it contrast?

9. _____

_____

_____

The result of our sin is a spiritual separation from God. We deserve death, but God freely gives us eternal life through Jesus Christ. To do this, God had to deal with the issue of our sin. To see how He did this, turn to *Isaiah 53:6* and summarize the verse below.

10. _____

BUT _____

In the Old Testament, the Jewish people expressed their faith in God's forgiveness of sin through animal sacrifices. The sins of the people would be symbolically placed on an animal such as an unblemished lamb. This animal became the substitute for the people. Following the same pattern, *Isaiah 53:6* says that God would cause our sins to be placed on Jesus, who is the Messiah spoken of in this passage. While the animal sacrifices were temporary, Jesus would be the ultimate and permanent substitute for us. For further study about Jesus as our sacrifice and substitute, you can read *John 1:29*, as well as *Hebrews 7:27; 9:12, 28,* and *10:10* on your own.

BUT GOD, BEING RICH IN MERCY

We find another great contrasting "but" in *Romans 5:6-8*. Summarize the contrast expressed by the "but" in *verse 8*.

11. We were _____

_____

But God _____

_____

This is a powerful example of love. God had to deal with our sin completely; He couldn't just brush it aside. So when He provided a permanent substitute, the substitute had to die in our place. When Jesus died on the cross, He accomplished everything we needed to restore our relationship to God. He offers the way to remove the penalty and power of sin from our lives. He offers us forgiveness and a new life to live on earth, victory over death, and the promise of an eternal life with the Father. When we receive the gift referenced in *Romans 6:23*, we are no longer separated from God, but are brought near by Jesus' blood *(Ephesians 2:13)*. Jesus' sacrifice accomplished all these things once and for all.

God's gift of salvation is freely offered to all of us. If we believe this and receive Him as that sacrifice for our own sin, then we have eternal life. We do not earn it, and we do not deserve it. We can never be good enough to meet God's standards on our own or to pay the penalty for our own sin. We just gratefully receive the forgiveness that Christ paid for.

So each one of us must ultimately answer the question: have I received the gift of eternal life that is freely available to me? If you are not sure about whether you have responded to the "but" in the middle of *Romans 6:23,* be sure to talk with your group leader or with another believer about it.

OUR RESPONSE

So let's personalize this idea of a substitute. Has anyone ever been a substitute or made a sacrifice for you in some way? Maybe someone attended an event/meeting in your place. Perhaps you received an organ transplant. Maybe someone took a consequence that you deserved. Think of an example from your own life. How did someone sacrifice or substitute for you?

12. _____

_____

_____

_____

BUT GOD, BEING RICH IN MERCY

What was your response to that person?

13. _____

_____

_____

_____

Most likely, your response involved love and appreciation. If the act was something significant, you probably feel like you can never repay it. Their sacrifice might have changed your life in some way. You may have gained a different perspective. Or you might have taken on the same causes as the one who sacrificed for you. The same is true about our walk with the Lord.

Read *1 John 4:19*. How does God's love change us?

14. _____

_____

_____

Our response to God's tremendous sacrifice should be that we accept that gift and live for Him out of gratitude. Love becomes our motivation — not fear, not appeasement, not somehow trying to carry out our part of a bargain. God's love is the motivation for us to love Him in return.

Now look at *verses 20* and *21*. What *should* and *should not* be a characteristic of a believer?

15. _____

_____

_____

Notice that there are no exceptions to God's command to love our brother. And there are no restrictions or conditions on whom we are supposed to love. Just in case there is any doubt, Jesus gave us a broad definition of our neighbor in the parable of the good Samaritan. He also commanded us to love our enemies *(Matthew 5:43-46)*. Our brother may be inconvenient to love or hard to love. People may be indifferent or even do evil toward us. Nevertheless we are to love, even as Jesus loved (read *John 13:34, 15:12,* and *Ephesians 5:2* for background on your own).

You might be having struggles right now. You might have relationship problems with others. You might be discouraged. But you are most fulfilled when you continue to love others (even in the difficult circumstances) out of gratitude for God's forgiveness. You start by accepting God's gift of salvation. When you do, God gives you the power to live His way by His Holy Spirit. He is the one who gives you the ability to love the way God loves. This is why receiving the gift of salvation through Jesus Christ can be so transformative in a person's life.

BUT GOD, BEING RICH IN MERCY

As we close, think about something that you have learned or been reminded of in this lesson and note that in the space below.

16. _____

_____

_____

_____

_____

_____

In light of all that you have learned so far (or have been reminded of), thank the Lord for His amazing love, grace, and mercy. Then ask for His strength and wisdom to live for Him out of a loving response to what He has already done. And finally, think about practical ways you can love your family, acquaintances, and even strangers.

In the next lesson, we'll see how Adam and Eve dealt with the original "but" and how their situation applies to our own responses to temptation. So prepare to be challenged spiritually and to be encouraged. Although your circumstances may not be the same, the biblical principles that apply are just as relevant today as they were thousands of years ago.

LESSON 2

"BUT FROM THE TREE OF THE KNOWLEDGE OF GOOD AND EVIL"
- DEALING WITH TEMPTATION -
(FROM GENESIS 2:17)

INTRODUCTION

We learned in Lesson 1 that, although circumstances today are different from those in biblical times, the human heart is still the same. Did biblical characters exhibit jealousy? deceit? greed? anger? fear? compassion? faithfulness? love? As we will see, the answers are all "yes." The Bible remains timeless and relevant because it deals with our responses to real-life situations. Most importantly, it addresses our relationship to God and others.

As explained in the beginning of this study, we will look at various situations in the Bible using the word "but" as a starting point. "But" can be a convenient way of identifying pivotal moments, warnings, and choices people made, for good or for ill. We can learn a great deal from these moments. In them, we find conviction, encouragement, hope, and biblical principles that we can apply in our own lives.

A SIMPLE WARNING

Let's continue our study of "buts" by looking at *Genesis Chapter 2*. Having completed the creation of the heavens and earth, God created the first man. Adam was distinct from the animals because he was created in God's image. This means that:

- He had a soul and could have a relationship with God, and
- He was given the ability to make moral choices.

BUT FROM THE TREE OF THE KNOWLEDGE OF GOOD AND EVIL

It also meant that he would have responsibility. Read *Genesis 2:15-17*. What was the job God gave Adam in *verse 15?*

1. _____

_____

_____

God had always intended for man to work. We often have the idea that Adam just wandered around the garden, munching on fruit from the nearest tree, with nothing much to do. Actually, he had an important responsibility, a God-given job to keep him busy.

While Adam did have a lot of freedoms, he was given one clear command in *verse 17*. Fill in the blank and summarize the command.

2. "But _____

_____

God's one command was so that Adam could exercise his created ability to choose. God wasn't trying to trick him. Rather, it was an opportunity for Adam to show his love for his Creator through obedience. With the command, God also told Adam ahead of time what the consequences would be if he ate from the tree of the knowledge of good and evil. According to *Genesis 2:17,* what was this consequence?

3. _____

_____

This included physical and spiritual death (separation from God) *(1 Corinthians 15:22)*. If he disobeyed, there would be a break in the perfect relationship Adam had with the Lord.

WARNINGS IN OUR LIFE TODAY

We'll come back to Adam (and Eve) shortly, but let's stop and consider warnings for a minute. There are many other warnings for us in the Scriptures. Read the following passages and list the examples of warnings.

4. Proverbs 24:1 _____

Matthew 6:1 _____

1 John 2:15-17 _____

BUT FROM THE TREE OF THE KNOWLEDGE OF GOOD AND EVIL

Think of some warnings that a parent might give to children, using the word "but." What can you think of?

5. _____

_____

_____

_____

These warnings are not because the parent wants to make the children's lives miserable, but because the parent loves the children and wants to keep them from harm. It is the same way with God. The Lord knew what was best for Adam, and He knows what is best for us. His warnings point us toward the choice to do good.

Unlike parents, however, God gives those commandments with perfect love. We can be confident in this because of who He is. Turn to *James 1* and read *verse 17*. What does this say about God's character?

6. _____

_____

Now read *Psalm 145:17*. How does God deal with us?

7. _____

_____

_____

God does not become impatient and He does not act capriciously. We may not always understand His purpose in giving certain commandments (or why He allows certain things to happen in our lives), but we can completely trust in His perfect love and goodness.

EVE AND HER ENCOUNTER

Now let's turn back to Genesis. In *Genesis 2:20-25*, we read how and why God created Eve. Lets pick up in *Chapter 3* concerning Eve's encounter with the serpent. Read *verses 1-7*. In *verse 1*, how did the serpent start the conversation?

8. _____

_____

What might the serpent have been trying to get Eve to do?

9. _____

_____

_____

BUT FROM THE TREE OF THE KNOWLEDGE OF GOOD AND EVIL

He certainly wasn't trying to get information so that he too could follow God's commands. He was trying to have Eve question what God had said. Satan used the same tactic with Jesus Himself as He was fasting in the wilderness *(Matthew 4:1-11)*. How did Eve respond in *verses 2-3?*

10. _____

_____

_____

Whether Eve heard the command from Adam or directly from the Lord we do not know. But we know that she was aware of the commandment, including the "but." She seemed to understand the warning. However, she added a few extra words to what God had said. What did she add?

11. _____

_____

Eve added her own ideas to God's word. This is something that we are inclined to do even today — adding little extra requirements and prohibitions that God never gave. The Pharisees did the same thing in Jesus' day (see *Luke 11:42-46* for an example).

The serpent then directly challenged what God had said. What did he accuse God of in *Genesis 3:4-5?*

12. _____

_____

At first, Satan asked Eve a seemingly innocent question (with a slight exaggeration). He was accusing God of lying and of preventing Eve from having a full, complete life. The serpent made this all sound so logical and plausible. Notice he never overtly said, "Eat this!" Rather he planted thoughts and doubts and Eve did the rest of the work. What should she have said at this point?

13. _____

_____

_____

If you have time, you can turn to *Matthew 4:3-10* and read those verses. When Jesus was tempted three times, what was His response each time?

14. _____

_____

_____

Eve could have said something similar to Jesus' response. "This is what God says, and I need to obey it." Instead, Eve's curiosity was piqued and she started to observe and test the fruit. She succumbed to three types of temptations. They are spoken about in *1 John 2:16*. What are they? Match these with the three observations Eve made in *Genesis 3:6.*

BUT FROM THE TREE OF THE KNOWLEDGE OF GOOD AND EVIL

TYPES OF TEMPTATIONS (1 JOHN 2:16)	EVE'S OBSERVATIONS (GENESIS 3:6)
15.	

THE FALLOUT

After eating, Eve gave the fruit to Adam also, and he made no objections. They were both responsible and they knew it. We see their response immediately after. Read *Genesis 3, verses 7-8*. Think of something you might do when you know you've done something wrong.

16. _____

_____

You might have said that you cover up your sin or mistake. Adam and Eve tried to do the same by hiding from the Lord. Do you think God, the Creator of the universe, was unable to find where Adam and Eve were? It is like small children when they think they can hide from their parents by covering their own eyes. "I can't see them, so they must not be able to see me." What was the real motivation for hiding, as expressed in *verse 10?*

17. _____

_____

With each question God asked (in *verse 11*), the inadequacy of Adam's and Eve's excuses becomes more apparent. What was Adam's accusation and excuse in *verse 12?*

18. _____

_____

What was Eve's excuse in *verse 13?*

19. _____

_____

BUT FROM THE TREE OF THE KNOWLEDGE OF GOOD AND EVIL

The one sin began to spiral into other sins. Adam blamed God for giving him Eve. Eve blamed the serpent. What began as a simple "but" in *Genesis 2:17* ended with what is called "the fall of man." Read a description of this in *Romans 5:12*. What was the result of the one man Adam's sin?

20. _____

_____

_____

Adam's disobedience didn't just affect him; we are all born dead in sin and have inherited a sin nature as a result. All of us struggle with the same things that they did at the very beginning — envy, pride, hiding our sin, blame-shifting, etc.

But here is our great hope today: we don't have to be trapped by our sin. God sent Jesus to overcome sin and death. He undid everything that began with Adam. *Romans 5* provides a thorough contrast between Adam's sin and Jesus' work. Through Adam we inherited sin and death. Through the gift of Jesus, we have righteousness and life.

The remainder of *Genesis 3* is then about the consequences of Adam and Eve's sin. What were some of the consequences?

21. *verse 16* _____

verses 17-19 _____

verse 23 _____

Think of the intense sorrow and regret that Adam and Eve experienced. Their fellowship with God was broken. They had known perfection but now they would no longer have perfect joy, peace, and contentment. They had paradise but now everything would become toil, difficulty, and pain. It is a tragic story, and we will see in the next lesson that they will experience the grief of losing their sons as well.

If we only read Adam and Eve's story, it would seem fairly hopeless. But we know that it is only the first part of God's plan for our redemption. Adam and Eve lost everything for a false promise and momentary pleasure. But Jesus gave up everything so that we could be restored to a right relationship with the Father, and will one day be perfected.

So let's look at what we can learn from Adam and Eve.

APPLICATION FOR US TODAY

Each lesson in the *Buts of the Bible* study will have a section on application to our lives. Why is this important? Look up *James 1:22-25*. Read *verse 22* and fill in these blanks.

22. *God says that we are not to just* _____ *the Word,*

but to also _____

BUT FROM THE TREE OF THE KNOWLEDGE OF GOOD AND EVIL

What do *verses 22-24* say about the person who only hears?

23. _____

_____

In contrast, what does *verse 25* say is the result for the doer?

24. _____

_____

God doesn't give us arbitrary commands just to see if we will do them. Rather, He intends them as a way for us to honor Him, and for us to be blessed by Him. In other words, **God's commands are for His glory and for our good**. As Christians, we show our gratitude and love for the Lord by doing His Word *(John 14:15; 1 John 2:5-6)*. When we do, He receives glory. In turn, we also reap the tremendous reward of the fruitful, abundant life that God intended for us *(Psalm 1:3; 19:11; Luke 11:28)*.

There are many applications we could draw from the story of Adam and Eve. What everyday temptations can you think of that are similar to the one that they faced? There are many examples, but just list a couple.

25. _____

_____

_____

One common temptation we all face is coveting or greed. We are tempted to covet in many ways: material possessions, jobs, relationships, etc. Temptations to covet are all around us. Advertisers spend billions every year trying to convince us to desire and buy things we don't really need. It is not inherently wrong to have material things but it is wrong when we become dissatisfied without them.

The serpent used this strategy with Eve. What did he seek to make her discontent with?

26. _____

_____

Satan certainly made Eve discontent with not having the fruit, as well as with not being like God. But he also made her discontent with God's way and plan. Many times, we also can become discontent with the plan that God has for us. We often think we are missing out on something, or that we won't be truly happy if we follow God's way.

Yet God is our creator and He knows the best way for us to live. When we are doers of His Word, we give Him glory and we also experience His blessings and promises. His blessing does not mean that He will financially prosper us or give us everything we request. In fact, we might go through even more trials. But we will have peace, joy, and wonderful fellowship with the Lord, and grow to be more like Christ *(Romans 8:29; James 1:3-4)*. We also avoid many painful consequences by going God's way.

BUT FROM THE TREE OF THE KNOWLEDGE OF GOOD AND EVIL

Think about this example of coveting. God tells us very directly not to covet in the Ten Commandments *(Exodus 20:17)*. Coveting might not seem all that bad because it is usually just in our thoughts. But when we covet, we are questioning whether God has really provided enough.

So why is this command important? What is the blessing or benefit of following it?

27. _____

_____

_____

If you want to study more about coveting and contentment, the Apostle Paul wrote about how to have contentment in *Philippians 4:10-13*. This is a great passage of hope for us. You can read these verses in your own study time.

There are many other commands God gave that can often go against our nature and our feelings. Remember in the previous lesson, we looked at *Isaiah 55:8-9*. God's thoughts and His ways are higher than ours. We might not understand the reason for some of God's commands, but His way will result in our blessing. When we choose to obey, we are essentially saying, "Lord, Your way is better than mine. I might not see it at the moment, but I will trust that You will do what is best."

In applying this to your own life, is there an area of your life where you have a clear warning from God, but you are tempted to ignore it like Adam and Eve did? You can write it down here (but you don't have to if it should be kept private).

28. _____

_____

_____

_____

_____

Ask for His help in this area. It may not be easy to obey the Lord's command, but we can trust the Lord because He is loving, and He intends the best for us. If you are a believer in Jesus, know that you have His Holy Spirit, who can give you wisdom and strength to do God's will.

Also recognize that, if you have not put your trust in Jesus Christ as your Savior, you do not have God's Holy Spirit in you to help overcome temptation. If that is the case, you have an opportunity to make that decision now. So go to your group leader or a Christian friend to find out more about making that decision. The end of Lesson 1 explains what is involved in becoming a Christian.

In Lesson 3, the next "but" will cover the relationship between two brothers: Cain and Abel.

LESSON 3

"BUT FOR CAIN AND HIS OFFERING"
- A LESSON ON FALSE SPIRITUALITY -
(FROM GENESIS 4:5)

SUMMARY OF LESSON 2 AND INTRODUCTION

In the last lesson, we saw how temptations we face today are very similar to those that biblical characters faced. The circumstances might be different, but the issues of the heart are still the same. We saw this with Adam and Eve, as they doubted God's character and His command, and even tried to excuse away their sin. We deal with these same things, but we also have great hope to overcome those temptations.

In this lesson, we move on to a new character, Cain. But let's begin with a question. When someone uses the phrase "going through the motions," what do they usually mean?

1. _____

_____

_____

Give an example of a situation where someone might be going through the motions.

2. _____

_____

_____

In effect, going through the motions indicates that we would prefer to do things our own way, and our hearts are not really in what we are doing. It is important to note that this is different from when we may not feel like doing something but we do it anyway because we know it is the responsible thing to do. There are many things we might not feel like doing at certain times (getting out of bed, going to school, going to work, fixing meals, cleaning the house, disciplining the children, etc.), but we know it's the responsible, loving thing to do. These would not be going

BUT FOR CAIN AND HIS OFFERING

through the motions. We will talk about this important distinction as we go through the lesson. We will find, however, that Cain was going through the motions of spirituality, and the evidence will come out in our Scripture passages.

CAIN CHOOSES HIS OWN PATH

Let's look at Cain. What do we know about him? Read *Genesis 4:1-3.*

3. _____

_____

_____

It is interesting to note that the Hebrew word translated "ground" in *verse 2* is *adamah,* which is the same word used for the ground in *Genesis 2:7.* From this *adamah,* God formed the first man, hence his name, "Adam."

Cain and Abel were both engaged in labor, each having a different job. Cain's job as a tiller is the same job of cultivating that God gave to Adam *(Genesis 2:15).* What was Abel's occupation?

4. _____

Read *Genesis 4:3-4.* Even this early in the Bible, offerings were already practiced. The Old Testament laws had not been given at this point. Yet both Cain and Abel knew what to do. Each brother brought an offering from his own area of expertise.

In *verse 4,* we see that Abel's offering was pleasing to the Lord. What is a characteristic of Abel's offering that set it apart from Cain's?

5. _____

_____

_____

The verse also says that Abel brought of the fat portions. This can also be translated that he offered the fattest sheep. There are important distinctions between the two offerings. The issue wasn't that Abel brought a sheep and Cain brought vegetables. The Bible does not say that God had any requirements for the offerings. The matter was not the *type* of offering, but the *quality.* Abel brought the first and the best, and this revealed his heart.

BUT FOR CAIN AND HIS OFFERING

God would later give specific instructions for sacrifices, starting with the Passover, and then in the actual Law. The Bible mentions many types of offerings — bulls, sheep, goats, birds, grains, and spices. This would be a separate study in itself, but one thing was consistent among the offerings: God commanded the givers to bring their best. Read *Exodus 12:1-5* for instructions given at the first Passover. What were the specifications for the lamb in *verse 5?*

6. _____

_____

_____

Go back to *Genesis 4:5*. What does the word "but" indicate in this verse?

7. _____

_____

Cain had his own ideas of spirituality. What evidence do we have that Cain's relationship with God was not what it should have been?

8. _____

_____

_____

Read *James 1:19-20*. What can we say about Cain's response based on these verses?

9. _____

_____

A SAD STATE

Even though Cain did not have the book of *James* to read, he knew that he did wrong. He also experienced feelings of dejection as a result. Read *Genesis 4:6-7*. What does God say to Cain?

10. _____

_____

Clearly, Cain was not happy. When God asks *"will not your countenance be lifted up,"* He isn't saying that Cain would necessarily feel better if he did right. The idea of 'countenance being lifted up' *(verse 7)* can be compared to the relationship between children and their parents. When children know they have done wrong and are confronted with it by the parents, where does the child usually look?

11. _____

_____

BUT FOR CAIN AND HIS OFFERING

Eye contact (or the avoidance of it) reveals a lot about the relationship between people. When a child does wrong, he/she looks almost everywhere except directly at the parents' eyes. It is the same way with God. When we have a right relationship with Him, our countenance is lifted up so that we can approach Him without shame, spiritually speaking. Cain could not do that in his present condition.

Note: The issue isn't how Cain felt. Sin doesn't always make us feel terrible. Very often, we can feel good while we sin. Conversely, we cannot assume that, by doing right, we will always feel happiness (i.e. the emotion). There are many, many examples in the Scriptures of people who suffered for doing right. We can often feel miserable when we choose to go the Lord's way. Doing so might cost us time, money, or relationships. This might cause us sadness, but in spite of this, we can know that there is nothing that can hinder our relationship with the Lord.

Cain was apparently going through the motions of his relationship with God, making up his own rules, and expecting God to be pleased. Nevertheless, God was still gracious with Cain. He didn't say, "Well, you failed. I'm done with you." Instead, He told Cain that he was at a fork in the road and had a choice. God's instruction in *verse 7* contains the pivotal "but" for Cain (if your translation doesn't use the word "but," the idea of two contrasting choices is still conveyed). What does God tell Cain?

12. _____

_____

Sadly, Cain did not heed the Lord's instruction. Read *verses 8-9*. While in the field with Abel, Cain murdered him. What did Cain do in *Genesis 4:9* in response to the Lord's question?

13. _____

_____

Cain's rebellion against God went even deeper at this point. He murdered his own brother out of jealousy and anger. Then he lied directly to God, denying any guilt (as if God didn't already know the truth). And with a callous and contemptuous response of *"Am I my brother's keeper?"* he also demonstrated a clear lack of care for his brother's death. Likewise, our tendency is to deny responsibility and even to cover up our sin. We can often make things much worse for ourselves, as we layer sin upon sin.

What were the consequences of Cain's sin in *verses 11-13*?

14. _____

_____

From *verse 13,* does it sound like Cain was repentant of his sin? What was he most sorry about?

15. _____

_____

Again, we see that human nature is still the same, even over thousands of years. Just like Cain, we are often sorry when we get caught, and complain that the consequences are unfair. Can you think of any examples of this that would be typical of what we do or see in today's world?

16. _____

_____

_____

_____

FALSE SPIRITUALITY VERSUS RELATIONSHIP AND THE HEART

When looking at the story of Cain, we can tend to focus on his sacrifice wondering, "What did Cain do wrong?" But we see that there were many other areas that were not right in his life. The sacrifice was just a manifestation of other problems.

From *Hebrews 11,* we get a greater insight into the difference between Cain's and Abel's offerings. Read *Hebrews 11:4.* What was Abel's sacrifice an evidence of?

17. _____

What did Abel gain from this? (You can also read *verse 2.)*

18. _____

God does not merely evaluate the mechanics of an offering, or whether we perform certain rituals. Nor does He want us to present a good face. He looks at deeper things like our heart and our faith (you can read *1 Samuel 16:7* and *Matthew 15:8-9* for extra study). Jesus taught that the heart is the source from which all our deeds proceed (from *Matthew 15:18-19*). Cain's primary problem was not his offering. Rather, his offering was a sign of what was going on in his heart. *First John 3:11-12* (you can read on your own time) uses Cain as an example of one who was not a child of God. His hate and murder arose from his heart's not being the Lord's.

We do not know all the details of what happened with Cain. However, from *Hebrews 11:4* and *1 John 3:11-12,* we do know that he demonstrated both a lack of faith in the Lord, and a lack of love for his brother. He was making up his own rules, not following the way God had intended for him. In contrast, those whose heart is the Lord's would place their trust in Him, seek to please Him, and love others.

BUT FOR CAIN AND HIS OFFERING

Jesus rebuked the Pharisees for the same type of false spirituality. Read *Matthew 23:23-24, 27-28*. What were some of the things He rebuked them for?

19. _____

_____

Jesus brings in the murder of Abel in *verse 35*. What do you suppose he was telling the Pharisees by bringing this up?

20. _____

_____

Like Cain, the Pharisees went through the motions and looked good on the outside. However Jesus constantly emphasized that spirituality goes beyond external things. What are some ways that we can make up our own rules for spirituality?

21. _____

_____

_____

In contrast to false spirituality, God shows us what matters most to Him. Turn to the book of *Micah, chapter 6* and read *verse 7*. The prophet Micah asks a rhetorical question here, essentially giving an extreme hypothetical situation. "What if I gave an enormous sacrifice — more than required? What if I even gave my firstborn child to Him? Would God be more pleased?" The answer is no. Look at *verse 8*. What does God desire from us?

22. _____

_____

Sometimes we think that we can gain God's approval merely by doing all the right things. If we only looked at the verse where God tells Cain to do well, we might come to that conclusion. But God also desires a relationship with us. He wants our hearts and for us to walk in fellowship with Him.

We see the same thing in the New Testament. Look at *Galatians 6:1*. Paul gives an exhortation to a specific group of people. Whom does he address?

23. *You who are* _____

So who is a spiritual person? All you have to do is go back a few verses to *Galatians 5:22-25*.

24. _____

_____

BUT FOR CAIN AND HIS OFFERING

God says it is simply someone who is walking by the Spirit, and demonstrating the fruit of the Spirit in their lives. There's nothing mystical about it. It has nothing to do with accomplishment, or how long you've been a Christian. True spirituality is when someone is walking in relationship with the Lord, depending upon His Holy Spirit.

APPLICATION

Love, walk, abide. God wants us to be in ongoing communion with Him. When we are, *then* we will be able to know and do His will. We cannot have true spiritual knowledge and victory apart from Him. Furthermore, Jesus said that we are branches and He is the vine *(John 15:5),* which means that we cannot even survive spiritually on our own. But when we are connected to Him, then we bear *His* fruit. This is the evidence of a truly changed life.

Let's look at what God produces in us. Turn to *2 Corinthians 5:14-15.* What is the change that God makes in our lives?

25. _____

A completely different *purpose* in life is part of the evidence of a true relationship with God. Instead of living for ourselves, we live for the Lord. Many people can do good things, including people who aren't Christians. However, the Lord sees the *why* of our good deeds, and for whom we do them. For further study, you can read *Isaiah 29:13, Matthew 7:15-23,* and *1 Corinthians 10:31.*

In bringing his offering, Cain did what seemed to him a good thing. Likewise, the Pharisees appeared devout on the outside. They gave things to the Lord, but it was for show. They went through the motions, made up their own rules, and they ultimately all missed the point — the things that are more important to the Lord. Cain, in his lack of faith, did not give the best to the Lord. In *Matthew 23:23,* Jesus said the Pharisees neglected justice, mercy, and faithfulness (similar to *Micah 6:8).*

If they had been in a relationship with the Lord, walking with Him, they could have known what God was looking for. This is the challenge to us today. What does that relationship look like in our lives?

26. _____

_____

To answer that question, think about a good relationship with a friend or spouse. What is the evidence of a good relationship with that person?

27. _____

_____

BUT FOR CAIN AND HIS OFFERING

Does it involve how often you talk? your manner of speaking with them? willingness to listen and encourage? how you make decisions? willingness to forgive? Similarly, we cannot have a right relationship with the Lord without spending time with Him. We listen to Him through His Word and communicate with Him through prayer.

But since walking in the Spirit is key, and the fruit of the Spirit is the evidence of that relationship, let's think about what the fruit of the Spirit might look like in specific situations. Using the table below, list an example situation. Then write what the fleshly, self-oriented response might be. Then choose characteristics of the fruit of the Spirit (love, joy, peace, patience, kindness, goodness, faithfulness, gentleness, self-control) and write out how it might be practically applied in that situation.

Look at the first example done for you. Then, as a group, apply this to Cain's life. What could have been Cain's response? Finally, in the last row, apply this to your own life. What is a situation you have faced or might face currently? What is (or has been) a typical response? And what would be the response God would want you to have? You don't have to complete this during the meeting or discuss with the group, but it is a great opportunity for you to apply at home or with others what you have learned in this lesson.

EXAMPLE SITUATION	FLESHLY RESPONSE	GODLY RESPONSE (FRUIT OF THE SPIRIT)	HOW THE CHARACTERISTIC IS EXHIBITED
Someone unfairly criticized you at work	*retaliation*	*kindness*	*find ways to bless them (Romans 12:14). If there was a misunderstanding, try to explain*
Cain's life: Abel gets recognized for an accomplishment	*anger, jealousy*		
Your life:			

We cannot force ourselves by human strength or willpower to exhibit the fruit of the Spirit. It is a work of the Lord as we submit to His will and control. When we abide in the Lord, then we will fulfill His commands, bearing His fruit, and not our own. This is supernatural living.

BUT FOR CAIN AND HIS OFFERING

If we are in a difficult situation or relationship, we often ask our friends or family, "What should I say?" or "What would you do?" This exercise is intended to point you to the best Source we have for wisdom, help, and strength — God's Word and His Spirit. If you need some help figuring out how the Scriptures might apply to your specific circumstance, talk to your group leader or mature Christian family member or friend so that you might be able to seek the answers in God's Word together.

As we close in prayer, ask the Lord for wisdom in how to respond in difficult situations. You may not feel like responding in a godly way, but remember God did not promise us (or Cain) that His way would always feel good or be easy. Jesus, our example, did not want to go to the cross. Yet He entrusted Himself to the Father, praying, *"not My will, but Thine be done" (Luke 22:42; 1 Peter 2:23).*

May God give us the fortitude to walk by His Spirit in practical ways.

In the next lesson, we'll look at the "but" in the life of another character from Genesis: Noah. Noah's life contrasted dramatically with the direction of the world of that day, and there are many lessons we can learn from his response.

LESSON 4

"BUT NOAH FOUND FAVOR"
- LIVING RIGHTEOUSLY, WHEN IT'S NOT POPULAR -
(FROM GENESIS 6:8)

INTRODUCTION TO NOAH AND HIS TIMES

In the last lesson, we studied Cain's disobedience and his rejected offering. From it, we learned about *true* spirituality. God does not look at whether we perform certain rituals, or present a good face. He looks at the heart *(2 Chronicles 16:9)*. Rather than our own ideas of spiritual activities, God desires faith. Our deeds come as a result of and as evidence of our faith.

Our next "but" is in *Genesis 6*. Let's start by reading *verse 5*. Here we see several descriptions of man's character. What are they?

1. _____

_____

The situation was dire. Man's thoughts and intentions were set on evil all the time. It even caused God sorrow and grief *(verse 6)*. The Lord saw no solution but to wipe out most of humanity. And this is where the "but" comes in.

Read *verses 8* and *9*. What does the word "but" indicate in *verse 8?*

2. _____

_____

In comparison to the rest of mankind, Noah found favor with God. In *verse 9,* what does God's Word say about Noah's character?

3. _____

_____

BUT NOAH FOUND FAVOR

Perhaps you have been in school or in a job where people distinguished themselves from the others. Perhaps this was you. This person often gets labeled as the favorite, a "teacher's pet," or as an overachiever. What sort of pressures do you think are on this person?

4. _____

_____

_____

Noah was not a teacher's pet, as though he were someone who flatters or does all the right things to earn credit. He had a relationship with God. As someone who walked with God, Noah's life was in stark contrast to the rest. Genesis continues the contrast between Noah and the rest of humanity. Look at *verses 11* and *12*. What was happening?

5. _____

_____

Notice *verse 5* talked about the thoughts and intent of man. What is different in *verses 11-12?*

6. _____

_____

As we learned in the previous lesson, the heart is the source from which all our deeds proceed *(Matthew 15:18-19)*. Because mankind's heart was set on evil, it came out through their actions. And it spread throughout the whole world. The verse says that the earth was *full* of violence.

Many people think that mankind is basically good. Scripture, in contrast, indicates that every person is inclined toward sin. For example, we see this when we consider how we train children. Do children have more of a problem learning how to do what is right, or learning how to do what is wrong?

7. _____

_____

The answer is pretty obvious. Children are very creative in knowing how to do wrong. They spend their whole childhood, and beyond, going against their sinful inclinations by learning how to do what is right. We don't have to teach children how to sin; we come into this world with a sin nature. And in Noah's day, the nature of mankind was on full display.

God had been patient, but mankind had gone its own way and had thoroughly corrupted the earth. God was compelled to bring judgment on all of mankind, but He provided Noah with a way of escape. Along with His plan of destruction, God gave Noah instructions to build an ark *(verses 14-16)*.

Then, in *verse 18* we find the next "but." Read *verses 17* and *18*. What does the word "but" indicate in this passage?

8. _____

_____

BUT NOAH FOUND FAVOR

This "but" gives hope because it shows God's promise to Noah as opposed to His response to the wickedness of the rest of humanity.

We use "but" in similar ways today. Think of some of some hope-giving "buts" that we might use with others or in society today. For example complete the following sentences.

9. *Exercise is hard work, but* _____

____ *This travel time is very long, but* _____

____ *I'm not going to let you have that toy right now, but* _____

_____

NOAH'S CHARACTER

Lets turn to the single-verse commentary on Noah's life in *Hebrews 11*. We went to this passage in the previous lesson when we looked at Abel's sacrifice. Noah is listed among those characters who acted in great faith. In *verse 7,* what was Noah's demonstration of faith?

10. _____

How is this an act of faith? You can refer to *verse 1* if you need to.

11. _____

_____

_____

What does *verse 7* say was the purpose of the ark?

12. _____

_____

Because of his faith, what was the reward or end result for Noah?

13. _____

_____

Think about this: God told Noah to build a bigger boat than any other that may have existed at the time (it was half the length of a modern aircraft carrier). The boat was designed specifically for a flood, but rain hadn't started yet. It would hold animals, but Noah hadn't amassed any sort of collection. In fact, these things wouldn't happen for many more decades. His family members might have questioned what he was doing and why. Yet Noah still did it because he believed God.

BUT NOAH FOUND FAVOR

Genesis does not tell us what it was like to undertake such a project, but you can imagine the mockery that Noah probably endured. What do you think might have been some of the things people said, or what might you have said had you been there in the worldly crowd?

14. _____

_____

_____

_____

Even though things likely became difficult for Noah, we know that he persevered and obeyed the Lord over many, many years. His faith is recorded as an example for us. Let's look again at *Hebrews 11:1*. How is faith defined here?

15. _____

_____

What are some demonstrations of faith in our daily life? They can be small examples that we often take for granted.

16. _____

_____

_____

Remember that Noah was someone who walked with God *(Genesis 6:9)*. His faith and his action were based on his relationship with the Lord. He knew God's holiness, power, and provision. So he could place his trust in God's character, even though the command may have seemed daunting.

INDIVIDUAL RESPONSIBILITY AND RIGHTEOUSNESS

In *Ezekiel 14,* God used Noah as an example of righteousness. At the time when Ezekiel was a prophet, the people of Israel were far from the Lord. God told them that, even if they had Noah, Daniel, or Job (men of faith and righteousness), Israel would still be judged. The righteousness of these three would not cover the sins of the whole nation *(Ezekiel 14:14-20)*.

The point is that righteousness does not rub off from others. It is not automatically inherited from the family we are born into, bestowed by the church we attend, or achieved from experience. It can be observed and learned, but ultimately, righteousness is an individual decision about whether or not to believe that God's way for our lives is best and then to follow Him.

Individual responsibility before God is one of the themes of the book of *Ezekiel.* Turn to *Ezekiel 18:1-20.* There was a false proverb circulating in Israel in those days. What was it, in *verse 2?*

17. _____

_____

What did the Israelites mean in using this proverb?

18. _____

_____

_____

What was God's reaction to the proverb in *verse 3?*

19. _____

_____

_____

God explains His ways by giving the Israelites a hypothetical situation. *Verses 5* through *9* describe someone who lives righteously; he does not commit idolatry, and he deals justly and mercifully with others. This righteous man then has a son who is violent and oppressive *(verses 10-13),* who then has a son who goes the complete opposite direction from his wicked father *(verses 14-17).* What does God say about personal responsibility toward the end of *verse 17?*

20. _____

_____

What is the summary in *verse 20?*

21. _____

_____

Noah wasn't doomed to be like the culture around him, repeating their sins. Instead, he made a personal decision to follow the Lord, standing firm in his faith despite the unrighteousness of the world around him. God dealt justly with Noah, just as He dealt with the wickedness of the world.

How does the understanding of our individual responsibility toward God give us hope?

22. _____

_____

_____

It is comforting to know that we are not spiritually trapped by someone else's sin. But this is also a warning that we cannot blame someone else for our sin. We are accountable before God for our own decisions. God looks at each of our own responses to His commandments.

CONCLUSION AND APPLICATION

Noah was righteous in the face of tremendous pressures. He likely faced ridicule and cynicism. He might have faced setbacks, while those around him became prosperous by dishonest means. And he had to wait decades to see the actual purpose of God's command. It would have been tempting to give up, or to do things the ways other people were doing them.

BUT NOAH FOUND FAVOR

In looking at Noah's life, we should ask an important question: what is true righteousness and how do we attain it?

The Hebrew word for righteous, *tsaddiyq,* and Greek word, *dikaios,* both mean someone who is lawful, innocent, or virtuous in character. There were many characters in the Bible who were called righteous and blameless. This does not mean that they were perfect or sinless, but the overall pattern of their lives was of dealing justly, abstaining from worldly practices, and following the Lord *(Micah 6:8).*

*** OPTIONAL STUDY / DISCUSSION ***

When we are introduced to Noah in *Genesis 6,* he is described as righteous and blameless. Read *Hebrews 11:7* again. When does this verse say that Noah obtained righteousness?

23. _____

How is it that Noah was righteous *before* the flood, but then he *became* righteous by faith? How do these two ideas fit together? Is righteousness something that we do? Or is it only given to us by God?

24. _____

_____

_____

This is important for us to consider because it still applies to us today. Just like Noah, we are righteous by faith. Noah's faith was in God's plan of deliverance by the ark. Ours is in His deliverance through the work of Jesus — His death for our sin and His resurrection for our new life. When we place our faith in Christ, we are declared righteous before God. The English word typically used for this is "justification." For additional study, you can look up the following: *Romans 3:22; 4:5; 5:19; 1 Corinthians 1:30; 2 Corinthians 5:21; Galatians 2:16; Philippians 3:9.*

So then, is there a righteousness that *we* do? The Scriptures say that there is no one righteous *(Romans 3:10)* and that we cannot do anything good on our own *(John 15:5).* But they also say that we ought to strive towards godliness *(Proverbs 15:9, 21:21; Matthew 5:6; 1 Timothy 6:11; 2 Timothy 2:22).* Is this a contradiction?

Quoting Habakkuk, *Galatians 3:11* says that the righteous live (are justified) by faith. That is the beginning of our spiritual lives. But our faith doesn't end here. Look up the following verses to see the role that faith plays in our lives.

Look up *2 Corinthians 5:7.* What is the principle Paul gives here?

25. _____

_____

Read *Hebrews 11:6*. According to this verse, how is faith important?

26. _____

_____

Finally, turn to *Romans 14:23*. What is the principle here about faith?

27. _____

_____

It takes faith to do what's right. When God commands us to do something, it might not make sense at the time. For example, God tells us in *1 Peter 2:18* to submit to our employers … even the unreasonable ones. Why shouldn't we stand up for our rights? It doesn't make sense from a worldly perspective. But we have God's promises that we will be blessed if we follow His commands, that things will work out for the good, and that we will be more like Him.

*** END OF OPTIONAL STUDY / DISCUSSION ***

Let's apply to our own circumstances all that we've learned. What are some pressures that might test our faith in God's commands? For example, you might be asked by a boss or colleague to tell a lie at work, or you might be drawn into a conversation where people are gossiping or tearing someone else down. Give some other example situations or temptations.

28. _____

_____

_____

_____

So let's take the example about being tempted to tear someone else down. *Ephesians Chapter 4* presents the practical, biblical truths for how to deal with this type of situation. *Ephesians 4: 22-24* describes the biblical principle of "putting off" the practices of the former manner of life and "putting on" new, righteous practices in their place. Let's pause here and read that passage.

This is immediately followed with examples of biblical "put-offs" and "put-ons," describing biblical ways to change: from a life of lying, to a life of truth-telling; from a life of stealing to a life of working and sharing; from a life of tearing down to a life of building up; and from a life of anger and bitterness to a life of kindness and forgiveness. The emphasis of Scripture is to focus on the "put-on," and the "put-off" will usually occur as a by-product. In other words, the person who is angry toward another person should seek ways to "put-on" kindness and forgiveness toward the very person with whom they are angry.

So let's take the example of gossiping or tearing down another person. Using *Ephesians 4:29* as the basis, identify the "put off" and the "put on." Then just identify what might be a specific plan that someone could use to put that into practice. The second example has been left blank to fill in on your own, either as a group or individually at home. You can use an example situation or temptation from Question 28.

BUT NOAH FOUND FAVOR

PROBLEM	RELEVANT SCRIPTURE	"PUT-OFF"	"PUT-ON"	SPECIFIC PLAN FOR CHANGE
Gossip or tearing down	*Ephesians 4:29*			
Insert example from Question 28:				

The Biblical Counseling Foundation publishes a *Victory Over Failures Plan* booklet that goes through this biblical approach in much greater detail, should you want additional information.

We cannot do anything righteous apart from the Lord. Yet God also says that we are to pursue righteousness. It is not a contradiction to say both these things. Because righteousness is based on faith, it makes us completely dependent on the Lord. We cannot take credit for anything. We cannot make ourselves righteous before God, nor can God honor us when we follow our own rules instead of His. True righteousness is when we place our trust in His way alone.

Think about it this way. Let's say you are driving to a place you have never been before and someone gives you a set of directions. You place your trust in those directions. When you arrive at your destination, you don't think about what a good and knowledgeable driver you were. You acknowledge that the directions were true and accurate. Likewise, when we place our trust in God's commands, we cannot claim to have a righteousness of our own. We were simply following His direction, which causes us to be righteous, and the credit goes back to Him.

This truth takes a great deal of pressure off of us. God tells us that He will continue His work in us, to mature (perfect) our hearts *(Philippians 1:6; 1 Peter 5:10)*. We cannot change our own hearts. He only holds us responsible for doing our part: our deeds (thoughts, speech, and actions). To see this further, you can read *Jeremiah 17:10* and *Matthew 15:18-20* on your own.

May God give us the strength to look to Him for leading and to His wisdom for making Godly choices as we face the pressures of this world. We praise Him for His true, accurate, and hope-giving directions for life.

LESSON 5

"BUT THROUGH THE RIGHTEOUSNESS OF FAITH"
- WHEN OUR FAITH IS TESTED LIKE ABRAHAM'S -
(FROM ROMANS 4:13)

INTRODUCTION TO ABRAHAM

In the last two lessons, we read about faith, and characters in the "hall of faith" in *Hebrews 11*. How is faith demonstrated?

1. _____

_____

From Lesson 4, what was the evidence of Noah's faith *(Hebrews 11:7)*?

2. _____

In this lesson, we are going to see how Abraham demonstrated faith. In fact, he is the next person of faith mentioned in *Hebrews 11* after Noah. Though he is regarded as a man of great faith, we will see that Abraham also had some failures.

First, let's start with some background. Turn to *Genesis 11*. We are first introduced to Abraham in *verse 26* as Abram, the son of Terah. We see in *verse 31* that Terah and his family traveled from Ur (which was near the confluence of the Tigris and Euphrates rivers in today's southern Iraq) to go to Canaan. They settled in Haran (which is on the Turkish/Syrian border of today) and it was here that Terah died *(verse 32)*.

BUT THROUGH THE RIGHTEOUSNESS OF FAITH

THE COVENANT AND ABRAM'S FAITH

Before we get into *Genesis Chapter 12,* think about a time when you had to make a move or take a trip to a place you were not familiar with, or start a new venture that was out of your comfort zone. What challenges did that present, and how did it stretch your faith?

3. _____

_____

_____

_____

Read *Genesis 12:1-3.* In Haran, God gave a command and a promise to Abram. Summarize God's command.

4. _____

What was Abram to leave behind?

5. _____

_____

Where was Abram supposed to go?

6. _____

What was the promise God gave?

7. _____

_____

This promise was repeated two more times to Abram in *Genesis Chapters 17* and *22* (we will look at those chapters later in this lesson). This is sometimes called the Abrahamic covenant, and is referred to several times in the New Testament as well. These references include *Acts 3:25; Romans 4:13; Galatians 3:8, 29;* and *Ephesians 2:12.* You can read these on your own. We will learn more about God's covenant later in this lesson.

Going back to *Genesis 12:6,* we see that Abram and his family continued on to Canaan (this is the region where Israel is today). Notice back in *verse 1* that God did not give any specifics; He only gave the command to go. It was as Abram was traveling that God showed him the land promised (see *verses 1* and *7).* This was an act of faith — simply to go when God said to go.

Then we see a contrast. Read *verses 10-20* of *Genesis 12.* What did Abram do in *verses 11-13?*

8. _____

_____

BUT THROUGH THE RIGHTEOUSNESS OF FAITH

Would you describe what Abram did as a lack of faith? In what way?

9. _____

_____

_____

The Lord never commends Abram for this. Abram acted out of fear, and was trying to protect himself (at Sarai's expense!). Even though he is known for his faith, Abram sometimes did things his own way, sinning against the Lord and others.

We see in *verse 17* one of several "buts" in Abram's life. Here it is used to show the effects on Pharaoh's life. His whole family was struck with diseases, and Pharaoh knew it was from the Lord. Even Pharaoh knew that taking a married woman was not right, and he called Abram out on his giving her away and lying.

PHYSICAL VERSUS SPIRITUAL CONSEQUENCES

Most of us have experienced a consequence of someone else's sin. In Pharaoh's case, the Lord caused him and his whole household to experience plagues because of Abram's decision. Maybe Pharaoh should have checked the situation out more thoroughly. We don't really know. The Lord was merciful though, and He showed Pharaoh the exact reason for their suffering. Pharaoh could then deal with the issue quickly.

The Lord also showed grace and mercy to Abram. This was a very public sin, and even Pharaoh saw it as wrong. Yet Abram's family survived, and the Lord still honored His covenant. God made a promise, and He remained true to it. This speaks of the greatness and faithfulness of God and His forgiveness more than the greatness of Abram.

Sometimes our own sin or lack of faith can have physical consequences for others. Can you think of any general examples? You don't have to use an example from your own life.

10. _____

_____

_____

It is important to distinguish between the physical consequences and the spiritual consequences of an action or event. Remember from Lesson 4 what God taught through *Ezekiel 18:* even someone living in the middle of a difficult, sinful family situation can still be righteous. They may suffer physically because of someone else's sins. But spiritually, they are not doomed to repeat the same sins. God gives tremendous promises for those going through difficult circumstances. Look up *Romans 8:35-37.* What does God promise us?

11. _____

_____

BUT THROUGH THE RIGHTEOUSNESS OF FAITH

In *verse 37,* God says in *"all these things"* we have victory. What does "all these things" refer to? Look at *verses 35-36.*

12. _____

_____

This is great hope. We might suffer physical consequences from others' actions, but nothing can separate us from having a vital relationship with the Lord. Furthermore, we can have spiritual victory even in the midst of dire physical consequences. Someone living in extreme poverty, or who has lost a parent or spouse, or has gone through some other difficult situation can still have peace and joy, and become more like Jesus. This does not minimize how difficult these challenges can be. But our ultimate hope is not in the physical outcomes but in our relationship to Jesus, which can never be taken away. *Romans 8:28-29, 1 Corinthians 10:13,* and *1 John 5:4* are just a few of the promises God gives us about difficulties (you can read them on your own).

Indeed, the Bible has many stories about people who did wrong and suffered physical consequences (for example, Ananias and Sapphira in *Acts 5:1-11).* Very often we can believe that this is always the case, thinking, "He must have done something wrong. Look at what he is having to go through!" This was common thinking in biblical days. Read *John 9:1-3.* What assumption did the disciples make in *verse 2?*

13. _____

_____

There is a very important "but" in *verse 3.* Jesus refuted the common perception that sin was responsible for the blind man's problems. What did Jesus say was the real truth about these particular circumstances?

14. _____

_____

_____

We learn later that Jesus healed the blind man, and that was a very direct, noticeable work of God. There are many works of God that can be displayed in us even when circumstances don't seem to be going particularly well. What might some of those works of God be?

15. _____

_____

_____

Take almost any adverse set of circumstances. These are opportunities for us to display God's work in us. When things go wrong (from our perspective), those watching us expect discouragement, frustration, even anger to set in. If we respond the way the world expects us to, we lose a great opportunity to demonstrate the difference Christ makes in our lives. But if we exhibit peace, patience, and hope instead, they see a work of God right before their very eyes.

BUT THROUGH THE RIGHTEOUSNESS OF FAITH

Some might say, "This is impossible!" You know what? They're right! It is impossible apart from being under the control of the Holy Spirit. This might seem like radical thinking, but we should welcome these opportunities when they come, so that we can demonstrate this difference and give the credit to the Lord.

THE UPS AND DOWNS OF ABRAM'S FAITH

Genesis Chapters 13-14 tell us how Abram and his nephew Lot parted ways. The passage also details Lot's capture among warring kings and how Abram went to battle to rescue him. At the end of *Chapter 14* and the beginning of *15*, God reiterated His promise to bless Abram. Read *Genesis 15:1-6*. In *verses 2-3*, Abram was clearly concerned about something. What was it?

16. _____

What did God tell Abram in response in *verse 4*?

17. _____

_____

_____

In *Chapter 12*, God promised to bless Abram and to make from him a great nation. Here in *Genesis 15*, He makes His plans clearer to Abram. He would give him a son, from whom his descendants would come. What is Abram's response in *verse 6*?

18. _____

_____

_____

*** OPTIONAL STUDY / DISCUSSION ***

Abram's faith is referenced many times in the New Testament. As we saw with Noah, God saw Abram's belief as a sign of devotion and He credited Abram as righteous (justification). Let's look at a passage that further explains *Genesis 15:6*. Turn to *Romans 4* and read *verses 2-5*. Where does our righteousness *not* come from?

19. _____

_____

Paul was challenging a belief in the early church that certain works needed to be done in order to obtain salvation. One of these works was circumcision of the males. Circumcision was an act that God established in *Genesis 17*, and it later became a requirement in the Law *(Leviticus 12:3)*. It was something that set the Israelites apart from the other nations. So it was naturally an important part of the Jewish faith as a sign of devotion to the Lord.

BUT THROUGH THE RIGHTEOUSNESS OF FAITH

However, Paul argued that salvation was always by faith, both in the days of Abraham and in the days after Christ's death and resurrection. In the early Church, this was an important issue because many Gentiles were not circumcised. They were looked down upon and told that they had to fulfill that command in order to be saved (see *Acts 15:1*).

Paul uses the example of Abraham in *Romans 4* to refute this belief. He affirms that Abram was credited with righteousness *(verse 3)* and then asks his readers when Abram's justification occurred. Look at *verse 10*. Was Abram declared righteous when he was circumcised or uncircumcised?

20. _____

Paul was making the case that Abraham was justified by faith *before* he did any works of the Law. His circumcision came after his faith. Paul encouraged the Romans that righteousness is not the result of a ritual, nor is it inherited. Anyone who places their trust in the Lord can be saved *(Romans 10:12-13)*. Many other passages deal with this issue of justification by works or by faith *(Acts 10:44-45; Acts 15:1-33; Galatians 5:2-6; Colossians 2:8-11)*.

*** END OF OPTIONAL STUDY / DISCUSSION ***

So far we have seen that Abram demonstrated his faith in two ways:
- He went to Canaan when God told him to go.
- He believed God's promise of many descendants.

However, we also see that he failed in his belief when he gave up his wife and deceived Pharaoh out of fear. Abram's faith wavered again in *Genesis 16*. Remember in *Genesis 15*, God revealed the plan of His promise: giving Abram a son. Now read *verses 1-2* of *Chapter 16*. What was not happening and what did Sarah believe was the reason?

21. _____

_____

_____

It had been about 10 years since God's original promise and calling of Abram. They had not seen the promise of a son fulfilled yet. So they decided to formulate their own plans in order to make God's promise come true. Sarai devised a plan to make Abram have a son through her servant.

Have you ever thought that God was leading you to do something and then nothing happened? Were you tempted to just give up? Were you tempted to try doing things your own way? This is what Abram and Sarai were dealing with. It would be tempting to start to doubt and then manipulate circumstances to make it happen. And this is exactly what they did. As they grew older, the task seemed impossible. They still believed in God's promise, but they thought that they might need to help God along.

BUT THROUGH THE RIGHTEOUSNESS OF FAITH

We can often do the same thing with God's promises to us. If our plans succeed, we can deceive ourselves into thinking, "This must be the way that God wants to bless me." Or we can ask God to bless our way regardless. This is what Abram did.

Turn to *Genesis 17.* God once again reaffirms His promise to Abram *(verses 1-8)* and changes Abram's name to reflect this promise. Look at *verse 5* where God changes Abram's name to Abraham. What does God say this means?

22. _____

Then in *verses 9-14,* God gave Abraham specific instructions for circumcision for all his descendants. This would serve to remind them of His promise and would set them apart from other nations. In *verse 15,* He also gave Sarai a new name: Sarah. God was creating a whole new life for Abraham and his lineage. Now read *verse 17.* How did Abraham demonstrate his lack of faith here?

23. _____

_____

In *verse 18,* what was Abraham essentially asking?

24. _____

_____

In effect, Abraham was saying, "God, can you change your plans a little to fit mine?" Abraham already had a son, Ishmael, and he was asking God to bless his actions. God was very gracious and did promise to bless Ishmael *(verse 20),* but His specific plan for Abraham was to do something miraculous — something only He could do. He would provide a son through Sarah, even though she was 90 years old.

Let's pause and think about what we can learn from both Abram's faith and his lack of faith. God has given us promises as well. For example, He promises us that He will provide for our needs *(Psalm 34:9-10; Matthew 6:25-31).* Think of an example where we try to take care of our own needs instead of waiting for the Lord's provision.

25. _____

_____

Sarah also had trouble believing God's promise of a son in *Genesis 18.* In response to Sarah's laughing, the Lord graciously reiterated His promise and challenged their faith by asking, *"Is anything too difficult for the Lord?" (verse 14).*

We might have difficulty believing promises because we have probably had someone break a promise to us. Maybe we have broken our own promises. Yet we can have confidence in God's promises because He is a good and powerful God. Nothing is impossible for Him.

BUT THROUGH THE RIGHTEOUSNESS OF FAITH

ABRAHAM'S FAITH AND ISAAC

True to what God had said, Sarah conceived and bore a son by Abraham *(Genesis 21:2)*. A number of years after Isaac's birth (we do not know exactly how many), God provided another test of Abraham's faith. Read *Genesis 22:1-10*. What is God's request in *verse 2?*

26. _____

Realize that Isaac was God's promise to Abraham and Sarah. God wasn't only telling Abraham to give up his son, whom he loved. He was telling him to give up the promise of future generations and nations. What was Abraham's response in *verse 3?*

27. _____

_____

But Abraham also believed that God would still fulfill His promise and preserve Isaac's life. In *verses 5-8,* what are two things that Abraham says that show that he was expecting God to do something?

28. _____

_____

_____

Now read *Hebrews 11:17-19*. This passage provides more explanation regarding what Abraham had to believe regarding God's promises to him. What was it he had to believe?

29. _____

_____

CONCLUSION AND APPLICATION

Abraham received many large tests of faith. Some he passed. Some he failed. Yet he is still regarded as a man of faith for believing God's promises. We also see God's grace and mercy. Despite Abraham's failures, God still followed through on His promises. We can apply a great deal from Abraham's life to our own.

Think of some situations in our lives today that you would describe as significant tests of our faith.

30. _____

_____

_____

_____

BUT THROUGH THE RIGHTEOUSNESS OF FAITH

Now select one of those situations and identify a promise of God that relates to that situation. Try to find a Scripture passage that contains that promise.

31. _____

_____

_____

_____

What challenges do we sometimes have believing that God will accomplish what is best in that situation?

32. _____

_____

_____

_____

How could God use this situation in someone's life?

33. _____

_____

_____

_____

At home on your own, consider going through the same process with a current test of faith, and write down how the Lord may be leading you to respond.

34. _____

_____

_____

_____

_____

As we close, think about the many opportunities we have each day to trust God. Some are large tests of faith, and some we may regard as small. No matter what, they are all significant. We do not need to approach these opportunities with fear, but with the understanding that the great God we serve has our best interests in mind. He desires that we mature in our faith, and He finds many creative ways to help us do that. In the process, He can use us to show the world the difference that Christ makes in our lives.

LESSON 6

"YET THE CHIEF CUPBEARER DID NOT REMEMBER JOSEPH"
- A LESSON ON UNFAIRNESS -
(FROM GENESIS 40:23)

JOSEPH HAS A PROBLEM

How many times have we heard the words "that's not fair!" As a matter of fact, how many times have we spoken those words, especially in our growing up years? List some situations where people are particularly prone either to say those words or at least to think them.

1. _____

_____

_____

_____

In this lesson, we are going to see multiple examples of unfairness in the life of Joseph, one of the sons of Jacob, Abraham's grandson. How Joseph handled it has direct relevance for our lives today. In fact, there are so many things to learn from the life of Joseph, that we're going to take two lessons to get through them. Lesson 6 focuses on how to handle injustices or situations we believe to be unfair. Lesson 7 focuses on forgiveness and reconciliation.

Joseph's life was full of troubles from his early years. So to see how they began, read *Genesis 37:1-4.* How would you describe the relationship with his brothers?

2. _____

_____

What specific things seemed to lead to a worsening relationship?

3. _____

_____

_____

YET THE CHIEF CUPBEARER DID NOT REMEMBER JOSEPH

How would you describe the relationship with his father? Why was it this way?

4. _____

_____

_____

Jacob (whom God named Israel in *Genesis 32:28*) had a preference toward Joseph, and it was obvious to his brothers. Read *Genesis 37:5-11* where Joseph tells his family about two of his dreams. What did both dreams mean?

5. _____

_____

_____

Joseph may not have intended to alienate his brothers, but his dreams clearly did not improve the relationship. To make matters worse, Jacob sent Joseph on an errand. Read *verses 12-14*. Based on the strained relationship, how might the brothers have perceived Joseph's coming to them?

6. _____

_____

_____

The brothers, out of jealousy and hatred, devised a plot to get rid of Joseph. Read *Genesis 37:18-24*. There are several pivotal points in Joseph's life. The first of them is signified by the "but" in *verse 21*. The original plan was to kill Joseph and cover it up. How did this plan change and why?

7. _____

_____

_____

Imagine the pressure of this moment. The brothers were unified; they had both the murder and the cover-up figured out. Then Reuben (Jacob's first-born son through Leah) began to question the plan. There may have been other brothers besides Reuben that had reservations about doing this. The fact that they planned a cover-up shows that they knew what they were doing was wrong. But peer pressure is a powerful force, and it happens in a wide range of situations. Think of some examples of pressure to follow the crowd. What motives or fears might drive someone to go along with the crowd even though they know it is wrong?

8. _____

_____

_____

YET THE CHIEF CUPBEARER DID NOT REMEMBER JOSEPH

Now read *Genesis 37:25-28*. Which brother spoke up for Joseph this time, and what was his rationale?

9. _____

_____

LESSONS ON COVER-UPS

Read *Genesis 37:29-36*. Reuben, who was going to rescue Joseph from the pit, was unaware of the brothers' scheme to sell Joseph. To his dismay, he found that Joseph had been sold into slavery and taken away. So the brothers carried out their cover-up plan.

These events illustrate the inclination we have as humans to cover up our sin. We see it in politics, in business, and in personal relationships. The fact that we try to cover up our sin tells us a lot about ourselves. What are some of these things?

10. _____

_____

_____

The interesting thing is that we did not have to be taught how to cover things up. Even Adam and Eve sought to hide when they sinned for the first time. From our earliest years we knew how to devise cover-ups in attempts to avoid getting caught. We all probably remember times as a child when we did something wrong and tried as hard as we could not to let our parents know. The human condition has not changed over thousands of years, which speaks to why the Bible is still so relevant even today. God knows His creation all too well.

Turn to *Psalm 139:1-4*. What does this tell us about God?

11. _____

_____

This passage describes one of the characteristics of God: He is omniscient. He sees everything and knows everything. This is difficult to fully grasp but is a powerful truth about the Lord. You can also read *Hebrews 4:12-13* on your own time. It is a good reminder that our actions, even when they are not seen by people on earth, are intimately known by God *(Jeremiah 17:10)*. This can be a source of fear for those doing wrong, but also of comfort for those who trust in the Lord.

What are some of the benefits for the Christian of knowing that God is omniscient?

12. _____

_____

_____

YET THE CHIEF CUPBEARER DID NOT REMEMBER JOSEPH

For the believer, God's omniscience can both provide comfort and act as a restraint. When we are wronged or when others seem not to notice us, we can take comfort knowing that God sees even when others do not. Jesus taught that God's omniscience should affect the daily life of a believer. In *Matthew Chapter 6,* He used a contrast between the focus of the religious leaders of that day (the Pharisees) and how we should be as true believers. The following three passages use the word "but" to show that contrast. Read each passage and list the area of life Jesus is talking about.

13. *Matthew 6:2-4* _____

    Matthew 6:5-6 _____

    Matthew 6:16-18 _____

Notice the common phrase in each of these passages: *"the Father who sees in secret."* What is the overall lesson God is teaching us here?

14. _____

_____

_____

The Lord delights in our doing good without drawing attention to ourselves. Our blessing comes from Him and not from whether other people see us. Applying this today, we don't need to succumb to peer pressure or to try to impress people. God knows when we are choosing the right way to go, even if others should mock or make fun of us.

An understanding of God's omniscience should also act as a restraint from doing wrong. As a Christian, our obedience should stem from gratitude for God's love for us, as demonstrated by Jesus' sacrifice on the cross. But the fact that God knows exactly what is going on in our lives, including our propensity to sin, should be a strong motivation not to tell that lie, not to steal, not to harm another person, and so on. For Joseph's brothers, this is the part of God's omniscience that they ignored. It was not even a consideration as they plotted against Joseph.

Did you ever think of why we have so many video cameras now installed in stores, or so many security precautions? It is because we know it is human nature to sin and hide things. Shoplifters don't tell the clerk as they are going out the door, "I'm taking this without paying for it." No, they hide it to keep from being seen. Joseph's brothers apparently thought their plot would never be discovered, but God knew all along, and even recorded it in the Bible for all of us to read and learn from.

ANOTHER SET OF INJUSTICES

Now let's continue with Joseph's story in *Genesis 39.* Read *verses 1-7* as background.

YET THE CHIEF CUPBEARER DID NOT REMEMBER JOSEPH

Joseph was sold in Egypt as a slave to a government official named Potiphar. God gave Joseph success in Potiphar's house, until Potiphar's wife attempted to seduce him. Here we see the next "but" in Joseph's life. Read *verses 8* and *9*. What was the reason that he said he could not participate in this sin?

15. _____

_____

Joseph clearly understood God's omniscience and he recognized his privileged position. He respected his master and was determined to honor him, but more importantly, he knew that to lie with Potifer's wife would have been a sin against the Lord.

But Potiphar's wife persisted, and Joseph kept resisting. In *verses 11-18* (you can read them on your own), Potiphar's wife, rejected by Joseph, devised her own plot. When Joseph fled her advances, she grabbed his garment and claimed that he had taken advantage of her. Read *verses 19-20*. What was the injustice that was inflicted on Joseph?

16. _____

_____

What sort of responses are we tempted to have when we've been treated unjustly?

17. _____

_____

_____

_____

Read *verses 21-23*. With Joseph now in prison, what did the chief jailer (warden) do to him?

18. _____

_____

Joseph apparently had an exceptional testimony with the warden. Joseph didn't sit around feeling sorry for himself, but willingly took on the responsibilities given to him. His ascension wasn't just because he was a nice person. Joseph was probably recognized as trustworthy, hardworking, honest, and fair in the way he dealt with people and responsibilities. But what is also the reason for Joseph's success? Look again at *verses 21* and *23*.

19. _____

_____

This is important to remember in our own lives. Through unfair or difficult times, the Lord can still display His kindness and blessing to us. This may or may not involve physical success like Joseph, but we can have spiritual peace and contentment in spite of adversity.

YET THE CHIEF CUPBEARER DID NOT REMEMBER JOSEPH

Now read *Genesis 40:1-5.* Pharaoh's cupbearer and baker ended up in Joseph's jail, and Joseph was appointed to oversee them. Both of them had troubling dreams, which they told to Joseph. Joseph first interpreted the dream for the cupbearer, whose dream predicted a favorable outcome. Because Joseph knew that the cupbearer would be back in favor with Pharaoh, he made a request of him. What was the request in *verse 14?*

20. _____

_____

We know from *verses 16-19* that Joseph's interpretation of the chief baker's dream did not predict such a happy outcome as that of the cupbearer's. Now read *verses 20-23.* Here is another crossroad in Joseph's life, and a third injustice. What happened to him this time?

21. _____

_____

Being forgotten was no small oversight for Joseph. He spent another two years in prison after the cupbearer's release.

CONCLUSION AND APPLICATION

Think back through your own life. You probably remember one or more times that you have been forgotten or ignored. Maybe it was a raise in pay you thought you deserved. Maybe it was some kind of opportunity you expected to have, but never developed. Maybe it was someone simply not appreciating something you had done for them. Injustices will happen in life. People will forget about you at times. But here are some Bible verses to remember when you have been put in that position.

- *1 Corinthians 13* describes the characteristics of biblical love. At the end of *verse 5,* what is one of those characteristics?

22. _____

This is not easy. Our nature is to remember injustices, and even keep track of them in our minds, so that we can gain an advantage or even take revenge at some point. When we are tempted to do that, we can look to Jesus as the ultimate example of how to respond to unfair and unjust treatment.

- Read *1 Peter 2:21-23,* which describes how Jesus responded in the midst of His most difficult and painful trial. Following Jesus' example, what are we *not* to do?

23. _____

_____

YET THE CHIEF CUPBEARER DID NOT REMEMBER JOSEPH

The "but" in the middle of *verse 23* introduces what we *are* to do instead. What is that?

24. _____

_____

What is the attribute of God that is mentioned here that we can remind ourselves of?

25. _____

_____

It is in our fleshly nature to dwell on injustices. This only leads to holding grudges, bitterness, worsening relationships, and even retaliation. But God shows us His better way. We simply place ourselves under His care and control. He gives us the great hope that, even in very difficult circumstances, He is the ultimate judge of our lives and character.

We do not want to minimize the challenges of having been treated unfairly, perhaps even treated unfairly under the law. Responding the way Jesus did can be very difficult, and at some point the unfairness may need to be addressed. But our motivation as a believer should be to act out of love for the other individuals, helping them to learn how to treat others, not merely to defend our own rights. This is a huge opportunity to show the world the difference Jesus can make in our life.

As we close Part 1 of the lessons on Joseph's life, consider whether there are areas in your life where you are still holding on to injustices that may have occurred in the past. In light of Jesus' great sacrifice for you, you can let go of them and entrust yourself to Him who judges righteously. This can be a life-transforming truth and can, in turn, be an example to others. For further biblical truth on this topic, you can also read *Luke 6:35-36; Romans 12:14, 17;* and *1 Peter 3:8-9* on your own time.

LESSON 7

"BUT GOD MEANT IT FOR GOOD"
- A LESSON ON FORGIVENESS -
(FROM GENESIS 50:20)

INTRODUCTION

In the last lesson, we looked at a series of injustices that Joseph experienced, one after the other. Through it all, Joseph simply kept on serving the Lord right where he was. We closed the lesson by looking at how Jesus dealt with the injustices He experienced and how powerful His example is to us even today. In this lesson we'll see how Joseph, because of his faithfulness, was provided opportunities to serve the Lord even further. At the end of his story, we find a powerful lesson on forgiveness and reconciliation.

Before we get back to the study, here's a question. Think about young children in general. What sorts of disputes do they tend to get into? What can make them reluctant to be reconciled with their siblings or other children?

1. _____

_____

_____

_____

Children can often have disputes over things that adults would consider trivial. But to those involved at the time, the issues usually seem pretty important. In the case of Joseph's brothers, their dispute turned into jealousy, anger, and resentment, and it cascaded into something very serious. But we will see that Joseph was the one to extend forgiveness to his brothers. We will also see that there is a strong parallel between the story of Joseph and how God, through His Son Jesus, initiated reconciliation in the world.

BUT GOD MEANT IT FOR GOOD

SEEING AND USING OPPORTUNITIES

When we left Joseph's story, we saw that he was in prison, wrongly accused of assaulting Potiphar's wife. In prison, he interpreted the dreams of two men who served Pharaoh (a baker and a cupbearer). Sadly, Pharaoh's cupbearer forgot about Joseph, and he remained there for two more years. Read *Genesis 41:1-8* about a dream that Pharaoh had.

In *verses 9-13,* the cupbearer remembered Joseph and spoke to Pharaoh about Joseph's ability to interpret dreams. It was a little late, but at least he remembered. Read *verses 14-16.* What was Joseph's answer to Pharaoh about his ability to interpret?

2. _____

_____

Joseph never forgot that the Lord was the One who gave him his abilities. After many years of being enslaved and imprisoned, it would be tempting to be embittered and to think that any success was because of his own hard work. Yet Joseph's example is a good reminder for us to give credit to the Lord when He has gifted us in some way and to thank Him for what He has provided for us, regardless of how large or small that may be.

Now read Joseph's interpretation of Pharaoh's dream and his advice to Pharaoh in *Genesis 41:25-37.* Not only did God give Joseph wisdom to interpret the dreams, but He also gave him wisdom to outline a plan. Joseph gave Pharaoh instructions on what kind of person should oversee this plan. Read *verse 33* again. What should the qualifications of this person be?

3. _____

_____

This leads to the next logical question: Who should oversee this tremendous responsibility? Well, Pharaoh answered that question in the subsequent verses without Joseph's having to say another word. Read *Genesis 41:38-43.* How did Pharaoh describe Joseph's character?

4. _____

_____

Pharaoh saw Joseph as the perfect candidate for this new job opening. This could be one of the most remarkable promotions of all time — straight from prison to second in command. Certainly, the hand of God was at work to make this happen. But as you look back over Joseph's life, how do you think God used Joseph's trials to make him wise and discerning?

5. _____

_____

_____

_____

God raised Joseph up to have a great deal of authority in the land of Egypt. But this wasn't the end of Joseph's story. God intended to use Joseph's position for a specific purpose.

BUT GOD MEANT IT FOR GOOD

JOSEPH'S FAMILY COMES TO EGYPT

The famine came just as the Lord showed Pharaoh in his dream. It affected the whole region, and it brought many people down to Egypt (including Joseph's brothers) to buy food. In *Genesis 42:6,* the brothers came face to face with Joseph himself. Without recognizing him, they bowed in respect just as God had showed Joseph in his dream so long ago. Read *verses 6* through *12.* Joseph was speaking harshly to his brothers and was even toying with them a little. What would you guess Joseph's brothers were thinking during this encounter?

6. _____

_____

_____

Joseph asked several questions to learn about his youngest brother Benjamin. Desiring to see him, he sent his brothers back home loaded up with grain, but he kept Simeon in Egypt as collateral. This would compel the brothers to return with Benjamin. However, Jacob was reluctant to send Benjamin down to Egypt (as he had already lost his son Joseph, or so he thought). After some time of bargaining, Judah took full responsibility for Benjamin's safety, and they returned to Egypt *(Genesis 43:8-9).*

Now read *Genesis 45:1-8,* where Joseph finally revealed his true identity to his brothers. The reconciliation process began in *verse 5.* What was Joseph trying to convey in *verses 5-7?*

7. _____

_____

_____

The brothers' emotions had to be some combination of disbelief and intense fear. But Joseph comforted them with his perspective on all the things he suffered. There is an important "but" in *verse 8.* What does it show about Joseph's perspective?

8. _____

_____

_____

_____

LESSONS ON FORGIVENESS

Forgiving others can be one of the most difficult things we do. Many families, friends, businesses, and even churches have been split apart because of disputes and reluctance to forgive and be reconciled. This certainly could have happened in Joseph's family. However, Joseph saw the bigger

BUT GOD MEANT IT FOR GOOD

picture of God at work. He did not allow the various injustices or mistreatment to prevent him from forgiving. His brothers apparently thought Joseph would be justified in retaliating, judging from their fear of what he might do to them.

From beginning to end, the Bible is filled with themes of forgiveness and reconciliation. Joseph is one example for us, and our ultimate example is God's love and mercy through His Son's death on the cross for us.

So, what exactly does it mean to forgive? And what should it look like in our lives? The Hebrew and Greek words translated "forgive" have several other meanings including to carry or send away, abandon, or let go of a debt (that someone owes you).

In financial terms, imagine you owed someone a large sum of money (maybe $500,000). If the lender forgives that debt, it means that it is completely canceled. They do not just reduce the debt; you are at a zero balance. The borrower gains immensely; the lender suffers a loss.

In relationships, forgiveness means we do not charge the offense against the other. We do not mostly forgive and then hold on to small amounts of the debt. We do not ask for favors in return. God calls us to a radical life of forgiveness, in which we abandon and let go of the offense against us. This may mean that we suffer a loss.

Joseph certainly had a right to hold on to the offense of his brothers. He could have been merciful by just ignoring his brothers or simply withholding retaliation. Yet, as we will see, Joseph's forgiveness brought his brothers back into fellowship with him.

God expects the same from us. Even the Lord's model prayer in *Matthew 6:9-13* states that, when we request forgiveness of the Father, He expects that we forgive those who sin against us *(verse 12)*. God even tells us why we should forgive. In *Matthew 18*, Jesus told a parable to His disciples about the importance of forgiving others. As an introduction to this parable, read *Matthew 18:21-22*.

What do you think motivated Peter to ask the question, *"Lord, how often shall my brother sin against me and I forgive him?"*

9. _____

_____

_____

_____

Like Peter, we tend to place limits on how much we think we should have to endure at the hand of others. Now let's read the parable *(Matthew 18:23-35)*.

There are two significant "buts" *(verses 28 and 30)* that represent the forgiven slave's attitude toward the fellow slaves that owed him money. What do those "buts" signify?

10. _____

_____

_____

Keep in mind that a talent in Jesus' day represented over 15 years' worth of wages. That means the slave would have had to work for 150,000 years to repay his debt. A denarius, on the other hand, was worth only one day's wage. So what is the primary point of this parable?

11. _____

_____

_____

_____

Jesus is telling us that, even though we may have been hurt by others, it is small in comparison to our sin against the Lord. If He forgave us all our offenses, we should be willing to forgive the offenses of others.

Turn to *Ephesians 4:32.* Who is the ultimate example of how we are to forgive others?

12. _____

_____

What makes this such a compelling motivation?

13. _____

_____

In the parable of the debtor, Jesus likened our sin to having tremendous debt — a debt so enormous that none of us could possibly repay it. Yet mercy and forgiveness are part of who God is *(Exodus 34:6-7).* Because of this, He made a payment on our behalf to cancel out our debt. He didn't just overlook our sin; He sent Jesus to die in order to restore us to a right relationship with Him.

The slave's gratitude for the master's forgiveness of debt in the parable should have moved him to forgive the other slave who owed much less. Likewise, God's great forgiveness of our sin should move us to forgive those who sin against us.

Let's get back to the conclusion of the story.

Joseph invited his entire family to come live in Egypt to be saved from the famine. The brothers returned to Canaan and conveyed this incredible story to Jacob. His son was alive, living as a ruler in Egypt, inviting them to live in a land that would have everything they needed. Naturally,

BUT GOD MEANT IT FOR GOOD

Jacob had a very difficult time believing this story. Yet, desiring to see Joseph again, he went down with his whole family and they all resettled in Egypt. The children of Israel would remain there for over 400 years.

After Jacob's death, Joseph and his brothers went back to Canaan to bury him and to mourn. Read *Genesis 50:15-21*. With Jacob gone now, Joseph's brothers became concerned about something. What was it?

14. _____

_____

Joseph reassured them in *verse 19* and he asked them rhetorically, *"Am I in God's place?"* What did he mean by this?

15. _____

_____

Then in *verse 20,* we find the most famous and climactic statement in Joseph's life. The "but" shows us a stark contrast. What does this "but" tell us about God's character and His ways?

16. _____

_____

_____

_____

This statement of Joseph to his brothers represents one of the most powerful examples of undeserved forgiveness in the Old Testament and remains an example for us even today.

CONCLUSION AND APPLICATION

It would be an understatement to say that Joseph experienced many difficulties. He was sold by his brothers into slavery. He was falsely accused by Potiphar's wife. He was forgotten by Pharaoh's servants and left in prison. It would be easy for him to despair and to think that God had forgotten about him. Most of us would have said something like "this is so unfair!" But if there was one thing that Joseph kept in mind about God, what would you say it was?

17. _____

_____

_____

_____

_____

BUT GOD MEANT IT FOR GOOD

In our own lives, it is sometimes difficult to see how the Lord may be using any particular set of circumstances while we are right in the middle of them. Yet God says that we can be at peace and have joy in any circumstance, even when the situation seems dire or unfair. This is one of the marks of spiritual maturity. Joseph certainly had confidence that the Lord was in control through the numerous injustices he experienced *(Genesis 45:5-8; 50:20)*. He did not yield to the temptation to become angry or bitter or seek revenge. But, like Jesus, he entrusted himself to Him who judges righteously *(1 Peter 2:23),* as we saw in Lesson 6.

When you think about it, responding to unfair treatment in a godly way can be one of the greatest opportunities Christians have of showing the difference that the love of Christ can make in our lives. People often expect some sort of retaliation when they know someone has been treated unfairly or harshly. When that person responds in love and forgiveness, it can be a powerful demonstration of God's way. It is an example they would be unlikely to find anywhere else. This can open up opportunities for talking about the Lord that may not have been possible otherwise.

As we finish this lesson, there are two primary areas of application we can draw from the life of Joseph. First, think of a circumstance in which you are not content or that you are tempted to think is unfair. How can you entrust yourself to the Lord in that situation? How can you demonstrate your love for God and love for others through it? Prayerfully write down any specific actions you could consider for that situation.

18. _____

_____

_____

_____

_____

_____

_____

_____

_____

_____

Second, think of any individuals you have had difficulty forgiving. Put together a plan for how you could demonstrate forgiveness. A great resource to help you understand and demonstrate biblical forgiveness is the *Victory Over Failures Plan: Guidelines and Worksheets* booklet, available from BCF. It contains a set of biblical principles on how to carry out God's command to forgive in very practical ways. See BCF's contact information at the beginning of this booklet.

BUT GOD MEANT IT FOR GOOD

We all realize that there are times when forgiving someone can be very difficult. Sometimes the things that others have done may not justify forgiveness in human terms. The things they have done just seem too unfair and egregious. But this is also how Jesus could have thought about us. Yet He went to the cross anyway. May He give all of us the grace to handle injustice and offenses against us in a way that is honoring to Him.

LESSON 8

"BUT MOSES SAID TO GOD, 'WHO AM I?'"
- HOW GOD GETS OUR ATTENTION -
(FROM EXODUS 3:11)

GOD GOT MOSES' ATTENTION. HOW DOES HE GET OURS?

We saw in Lessons 6 and 7 how God used a faithful servant to achieve His purposes. Despite how badly Joseph was treated, how much he was neglected, and how unfair his life might have seemed, he kept on trusting the Lord for the outcome. Keeping God's sovereignty in view, Joseph extended forgiveness to his brothers, rescuing them from the famine, and providing a new home in Egypt.

Four hundred years later, the sons of Israel had greatly multiplied to the extent that the Egyptian leadership became concerned. The king of Egypt (Pharaoh) became so worried that he commanded the Hebrew midwives to kill all the male babies as they were being born. We see from *Exodus 1:17* why this effort was unsuccessful. Read the verse and explain the significance of this "but."

1. _____

_____

_____

When this plan failed, Pharaoh took even stronger action, commanding his own people to cast the male babies into the Nile River. One mother hid her baby for three months, and then set him in a basket on the Nile. Her intention likely was to have him float away from Pharaoh's cruel authority, yet God had other plans. The baby Moses was rescued by Pharaoh's daughter, and brought into Pharaoh's own family.

Turn to *Exodus 2:11-15*. When Moses had grown, he saw all the hard labor that the Hebrew nation had been forced to endure. He became angered when he witnessed an Egyptian beating a Hebrew slave *(verse 11)*. How did he respond in *verse 12?*

2. _____

_____

BUT MOSES SAID TO GOD, "WHO AM I?"

Even though Moses had been careful and methodical with his plan, people still knew about his action. Word spread and Pharaoh became aware of what Moses had done *(verse 15)*. As a result, Moses had to flee from Egypt to Midian (on the opposite side of the Sinai Peninsula).

Read *verses 23-25*. After some time, the king died but the Israelites remained in bondage. God heard their cries of desperation *(Exodus 2:24-25)* and He would soon set in motion all the things He had been preparing over the years. Meanwhile in Midian, Moses had been living a quiet life for 40 years, having married the daughter of a priest and become a shepherd. But his life was about to change.

Read *Exodus 3:1-7*. God used the miraculous phenomenon of a burning bush to get Moses' attention. While it is highly unlikely that any of us would experience this same type of event, God has other ways to get our attention. What might be some ways He could do this?

3. _____

_____

_____

_____

The Holy Spirit can use many different things to help us recognize a change we need to make, a person we need to encourage, a commitment we need to fulfill, or a relationship we need to work on. What are some things we can do to make sure this guidance is from the Lord?

4. _____

_____

_____

_____

One of the things we should always do is check that direction against Scripture. God will not lead us in ways that are inconsistent with His Word.

Even though God gave Moses an evident sign, Moses still made several excuses at first, and tried to make a case that he was simply inadequate for the job. Let's look at their interaction.

GOD CALLS MOSES AND MOSES RESPONDS … SORT OF

Read *Exodus 3:10*. What did God tell Moses about how He wanted to use him?

5. _____

_____

BUT MOSES SAID TO GOD, "WHO AM I?"

Now read *verse 11*. The "but" in this verse shows Moses' reaction. What did he say in response to God's plan?

6. _____

_____

What do you think he meant when he said, "Who am I?"

7. _____

_____

_____

Moses was overwhelmed by the task, and he implied that there were better people for the job. Most of us can relate to Moses' reluctance. We can often feel like we are unprepared or not the right fit to take on certain responsibilities. Think of some situations today where God could truly be calling us to take on a responsibility that we might be reluctant to do.

8. _____

_____

_____

_____

_____

Now read *Exodus 3:13*. This would seem to be a legitimate question, particularly in response to a voice from a burning bush. Moses may have been trying to confirm that this voice of God was the real Yahweh. He may also have been concerned that the Israelites wouldn't believe that the One True God sent him. Again, God didn't dismiss Moses' concerns, and His answer is one of the most profound statements about Himself in the entire Bible. Who did God say He was in *verse 14*?

9. _____

_____

"I am Who I am" is a statement of God's eternality. He has always existed and will always be present. Turn to *John 8:57-59*. What was the significance of Jesus' response to the Jews in this circumstance?

10. _____

_____

_____

BUT MOSES SAID TO GOD, "WHO AM I?"

Now read *Exodus 3:15-22*. God gave Moses a clear plan of what he should say to the Israelites and then to the king *(verse 18)*. He also gave him a realistic expectation of what he would face. We see this from the "but" in *verse 19*. What did the Lord tell Moses, and why do you think He told Moses that?

11. _____

_____

_____

The Lord said that the Israelites would listen to Moses, while Pharaoh's response would be very different. God forewarned Moses that there would be conflict. The way God prepared Moses illustrates how to train children for life. We can't tell them exactly what will happen in every scenario but we can explain some of the things they may face and how to respond in those situations. They will learn some of the lessons on how to respond from experience on their own (sometimes the hard way). But we can strive to help them understand situations from a biblical standpoint. Read *Deuteronomy 6:4-7*. When are we to be helping them learn about the love of God and His Word?

12. _____

_____

_____

In other words, these conversations can be part of everyday life. Whether we are at home or as we are traveling, God says we can use these as times to teach our children. We can talk about the day ahead or about a situation they are facing and how God commands us to follow Him in those things. The days can get very busy, but it is amazing how many opportunities we have to teach children a life lesson. List a few example situations where there might be an opportunity to teach a child a biblical lesson about life.

13. _____

_____

_____

Jesus is the ultimate example of biblical discipleship. He asked questions of the disciples, counseled them, and prepared them for a future that they did not yet understand. He did this constantly, throughout the day, using specific incidents as opportunities to teach, and He exercised great patience with the disciples in that process. So too, God was patiently preparing Moses for his future responsibility.

BUT MOSES SAID TO GOD, "WHO AM I?"

Now let's go to *Exodus 4*. After God outlined everything that would happen in Egypt, Moses posed another question in *verse 1*. What was it?

14. _____

_____

This also could have been a legitimate concern, but you can start to see Moses going down the path of what-ifs. In our own lives, we sometimes imagine possible scenarios in order to be prepared. Other times, we can ask what-if questions that are really just excuses. Provide some examples of what-ifs that could be used as excuses (note that some of the what-ifs could be excuses in one situation but not in others):

15. _____

_____

_____

In *Exodus 4:2-9*, God was gracious once again and answered Moses' concern. He explained in some detail how He would provide Moses with ways to help the people believe. God demonstrated various miracles to Moses, which he would repeat in Egypt. It's quite possible that the Lord showed him these miracles so that Moses would believe too! After God addressed his concerns, what did Moses say in *verse 10?*

16. _____

_____

Read *Exodus 4:11-13,* where God provides further assurance to Moses. What promise does God give in *verse 12?*

17. _____

_____

This is just like the promise in *Exodus 3:11-12.* When Moses said, "Who am I?" God didn't say, "Oh Moses, you're great. You have a lot of potential. You just need some experience." God said that *He* would be with Moses. God would accomplish those things by *His* power. Likewise, in *Exodus 4,* when Moses said that he wasn't eloquent, God didn't say, "Oh Moses, you'll do fine." Instead He said, "I will be with your mouth." God did not mean that Moses should just improvise or that he did not need to properly prepare. In fact, God counseled and prepared Moses before every single encounter with Pharaoh. From preparation to empowerment, God would make up for all that Moses lacked.

BUT MOSES SAID TO GOD, "WHO AM I?"

*** OPTIONAL STUDY / DISCUSSION ***

Turn to *2 Corinthians 12.* This chapter contains the passage in which Paul was dealing with a thorn in the flesh. It was obviously a source of great pain and difficulty for Paul, so he implored God three times that it be removed. *Verse 9* was God's response. God says His grace is enough for Paul. In the next phrase, God explained why it is enough. Why is that?

18. _____

_____

Then in *verse 10,* Paul said that he would boast in weakness, but *not* because it made him a better person. At the end of *verse 10,* what did he say was the result of his weakness?

19. _____

_____

Being content with affliction or physical weakness is completely opposite from the way the world thinks. Often our temptation is to avoid affliction at all costs. But God sometimes allows us to be put into impossible situations that we feel inadequate to deal with. These are the places that can best demonstrate God's power. For further study, you can also read *1 Corinthians 1:26-27.*

*** END OF OPTIONAL STUDY / DISCUSSION ***

Now let's go back to *Exodus 4* and read *verse 13.* This is the most telling "but" in this whole exchange. What was Moses saying this time?

20. _____

_____

And how did God respond in the first part of *verse 14?*

21. _____

_____

We don't know exactly what was behind all of Moses' questions and excuses. He could have felt inadequate. Perhaps he was a bit fearful of Pharaoh's reaction. Perhaps he just wanted to avoid what he knew would be a hard job. But at this point in the story, Moses was begging not to be given this responsibility. In effect, He was saying, "Lord, you don't choose very well. Someone else is better for this job." God was now to the point of anger over Moses' lack of faith. If we were in God's place, most of us would have said by now, "I'm done with you. You're not listening. And you're right, there is someone better." Yet once again, we see that God was gracious and He still intended Moses to be part of His plan. He answered all of Moses' questions and doubts and He again reassured Moses of His presence and guidance *(verse 15).*

BUT MOSES SAID TO GOD, "WHO AM I?"

MOSES GOES BACK TO EGYPT

After Moses departed for Egypt, he was joined by Aaron his brother. They faced the Hebrew people and did all that God had instructed. It turns out that Moses didn't have any of the resistance from his people that he had been so worried about. Just as God had said in *Exodus 3:18,* the people believed and worshiped God because He had heard their cry for help *(Exodus 4:27-31).*

On the other hand, the new leadership in Egypt met Moses with immediate opposition *(Exodus 5:1-4).* Because of Moses and Aaron's request, Pharaoh intensified the Israelites' work *(Exodus 5:6-9)* and things got tough for Moses. Read *Exodus 5:21-23.* Not only was Pharaoh resistant, but what did the Hebrew people start doing in *verse 21?*

22. _____

_____

How did Moses respond in *verses 22* and *23?*

23. _____

_____

_____

God had told Moses this would happen back in *Exodus 3:19-20.* In spite of Moses' complaint, the Lord again gently reminded Moses of His plan (see *Exodus 6:1-8).* He gave Moses the task of reminding the Israelites of His covenant with Abraham to give them the Promised Land. Moses met hostility from all sides when the Israelites refused to listen to him. He returned to God, discouraged and still doubting God's choice of a leader *(Exodus 6:28-30).* Once again, the word "but" is a strong indication of Moses' lack of faith.

The task that God gave Moses was immense. Yet God had been preparing him from the time he was a baby. In spite of Moses' perceived shortcomings, God was still assuring him and providing for him throughout the process. He supplied Aaron as a powerful assistant to Moses and He guided his words to the people and to Pharaoh.

You can read the rest of the story on your own. Pharaoh continually refused to set the Israelites free from slavery. So using Moses, God brought increasingly severe plagues on the land of Egypt. Finally, as God had told Moses, Egypt suffered the loss of their firstborn sons as the last plague, and Pharaoh conceded, allowing the Israelites to go. As you read through the story, notice how in the end, Moses did the talking, boldly challenging Pharaoh. This was evidence of God's growing him into his position of leadership.

BUT MOSES SAID TO GOD, "WHO AM I?"

CONCLUSION AND APPLICATION

Now let's translate the "buts" in Moses' story to our own lives. We have all had things that we were reluctant to do, but knew that we should do them. There might even be a situation in your life that seems daunting or even impossible. Think about a specific situation where the Lord has been getting your attention. You might want to revisit Questions 3 and 4 to be reminded of ways the Lord sometimes gets our attention.

This situation might not be a dramatic revelation or mission, but may involve a simple command of God. It might be a responsibility toward your family, or a friend, or toward someone at work. It might involve forgiving a person, or asking forgiveness. It might involve dealing with your responses toward people, like impatience or anger. You may use the space below, but if you need to keep it private, you don't have to write it down or mention it in the group.

24. _____

_____

_____

_____

_____

_____

_____

_____

It is important to remember that we cannot control the results or outcomes. Pharaoh let the people go, just like God had promised, but we don't have the same knowledge about how people will respond to our actions. We can forgive, but we cannot make another person respond to our request for forgiveness. We can exhibit the characteristics of love in *1 Corinthians 13*, but we have no guarantee for how other people will respond to our showing love to them. These might seem like little things in comparison to the story of Moses, but they are extremely significant in the sight of God and with respect to our relationships with others.

Our part of the responsibility can be summed up in *Luke 16:10*. What is that?

25. _____

_____

Notice the statement that the one who is faithful in a little thing "**is**" also faithful in much. The verse does not say "will be" faithful in much. In other words, being faithful in the little things is just as important to God as faithfulness in the so-called big things. Our responsibility is to

BUT MOSES SAID TO GOD, "WHO AM I?"

be faithful; God is responsible for the results, as much as we might like to control the results ourselves. It may be disappointing at times when people don't respond the way we had hoped they would, but understanding this principle also provides great freedom.

So, in light of all we've studied, prayerfully consider an action or actions that God might be calling you to take in the situation you described earlier. How can you depend on God's power to do it? Again, you can keep this private if you wish.

26. _____

_____

_____

_____

_____

_____

_____

_____

_____

_____

_____

_____

_____

You will have an opportunity to use this same situation in Lesson 9, when we learn more about how to overcome fear.

The story of Moses is a message of hope for us. The so-called little things can seem overwhelming for us to do at times. Even Moses, the leader of the Israelites, was reluctant and made excuses. In the face of a task he considered overwhelming, he tried again and again to get out of the responsibility. But God responded to his concerns at every step. And in the end, by God's power, Moses faithfully carried out the commission God had given to him. In the same way, when God gives us a command, He will also provide the power for us to do it, and we can rest in the fact that He is also responsible for how things turn out.

LESSON 9

"NEVERTHELESS THE PEOPLE WHO LIVE IN THE LAND ARE STRONG"
- A LESSON ON CONQUERING FEAR -
(FROM NUMBERS 13:28)

INTRODUCTION

In life, there are many times when our expectations come face to face with difficult challenges. We will see a biblical example of that as the Israelites get close to entering the Promised Land. Before we begin, think of some examples about these realities from our own lives. What situations can you think of where people start with high expectations but then realize that the work involved is harder than they originally anticipated? You can generalize and don't have to use a specific situation from your own life.

1. _____

_____

_____

_____

THE DILEMMA IN THE DESERT

We saw in Lesson 8 that, even though Moses was reluctant at the beginning, God used him in great ways to lead the Israelites out of slavery. Through Moses, the Lord displayed many powerful miracles in Egypt, and Pharaoh eventually let the Hebrew people go. However, the Egyptian army pursued them, and God again performed a miracle to protect His people. He opened up the Red Sea for them to pass through on dry land, and He closed the sea on the Egyptian army. After several months of traveling, the Israelites finally camped in the desert of Sinai, and God gave Moses His Law on the mountain. They would be there almost a year.

NEVERTHELESS THE PEOPLE WHO LIVE IN THE LAND ARE STRONG

At that point, the expectation was that God would lead them to the land He promised in His covenant with Abraham *(Genesis 12:1-3)*. In preparation, God instructed Moses to choose 12 men, one from each tribe, to serve as spies *(Numbers 13:1-2)*. Moses gave the spies clear instructions. Turn to *Numbers 13* and read *verses 17-20*. What were some of the things Moses told them to find out?

2. _____

_____

The spies went out as instructed, and after 40 days of investigation, they returned. Read the report of the spies in *Numbers 13:27-29*. What facts did they report?

3. _____

_____

In *verse 28,* there is a statement that transitions from the good news about the land, to the bad news. Some translations use the word "nevertheless," and some use the word "but." However, the essential meaning is the same: challenges lie ahead. Caleb, from the tribe of Judah, was first to give the recommendation based on those facts. What was his recommendation in *Numbers 13:30?*

4. _____

_____

We find the next "but" in this episode in *Numbers 13:31-33*. How would you characterize the majority report?

5. _____

_____

Now Read *Numbers 14:1-4*. List all the responses of the people that represent a lack of faith.

6. *verse 1* _____

   verse 2 _____

   verse 3 _____

   verse 4 _____

NEVERTHELESS THE PEOPLE WHO LIVE IN THE LAND ARE STRONG

It is easy to look at their response and think that the Israelites were shortsighted and untrusting. Yet the report of the spies and the reaction of the people clearly illustrate what can happen in our own lives. All of us have faced major decision-points (or even minor ones) that we knew could be a challenge for us. We might focus on only the negative aspects of a situation. We might even long to go back to the way things used to be because we see the task as too overwhelming.

Now take one or two of the situations you listed in Question 1 (or use a new one) and ask, "Why might someone be tempted not to follow through on this challenge?" You can use a situation you have faced as an adult or even from your childhood. Some of these situations can be very unexpected and difficult, and you do not necessarily need to write the selected situation down here, but if appropriate, you may choose to tell it to your study group. Part of this lesson will involve seeing how the Lord can use these types of situations and decision points to mature us in our faith.

7. _____

_____

_____

_____

It is one thing to decide *not* to take action out of prudence. It is quite another to be fearful, to complain, or to be consumed in self-pity like the Israelites were. Their fear led them to go against God's plans to bless them.

There is an important distinction we need to make here. This wasn't supposed to be a "should we or shouldn't we" decision for the Israelites. The Lord had already *promised* this land to them *(Exodus 12:25; 13:11; Leviticus 20:24)*. God told them the outcome, but they had to trust that He would accomplish it. They had to demonstrate their faith by going to battle, and God would give them the victory.

CALEB AND JOSHUA STAND FIRM

Not only were the people grumbling and angry with Moses, but they were at the point of insurrection. They were even calling to replace God's choice of Moses with a new leader who would help them return to Egypt.

NEVERTHELESS THE PEOPLE WHO LIVE IN THE LAND ARE STRONG

Here is an example in which the majority is not always right. It would be easy to get swept away by the tide of public opinion — especially when there is a multitude of angry and fearful people! However, Joshua and Caleb stood firm in their convictions. Read *Numbers 14:5-9*. What was their message in response to the people?

8. _____

_____

_____

Joshua and Caleb gave a strong yet gentle admonition to the people, reminding them of God's power to give them the land. They could have said, "Well, maybe this is God closing a door." Or "Why don't we just wait and take some time to talk through the issue?" Why didn't they say that here?

9. _____

_____

After Joshua and Caleb tried to persuade the people, we see a "but" in *verse 10*. It shows the final choice that the people made. What did they suggest at this point?

10. _____

_____

Have you ever been in a situation where the response was to kill the messenger? This is literally what was being proposed here. Let's say that you are in the position of having to deliver a difficult message. How could you present the message in a way that could help the receiver accept it? Keep in mind that the receiver may still not accept it, even if delivered lovingly, very much like what happened with Joshua and Caleb.

11. _____

_____

God gives us a command in *Colossians 4:5-6* about how to deliver a message. What is it?

12. _____

_____

He also tells us what our focus and conduct should be in *2 Timothy 2:24-26*. How should we be?

13. _____

_____

NEVERTHELESS THE PEOPLE WHO LIVE IN THE LAND ARE STRONG

Notice that these passages apply to how we address people who are outside the faith, not just fellow believers. *Proverbs 15:1* gives us another principle of communication. Summarize it in your own words.

14. _____

_____

While we can control how we deliver a message, we cannot control the way in which someone receives it. Jesus was the perfect example of gentleness and of graciously (but directly) speaking truth. Yet people refused to listen to Him; some even wanted to kill Him *(Matthew 12:13-14; John 5:18; 8:58-59; 10:30-31)*. God the Father still has plenty of people who do not heed His counsel. Joshua and Caleb were God's chosen spokespersons to deliver the right message to the people, and they did it faithfully. But they could not be responsible for how it was received. Even though we might deliver a message with grace and gentleness, the hearers are ultimately responsible for how they receive it. While we might be saddened by the response, we can have peace that we carried out our responsibility.

In *Numbers 14:11*, the Lord told Moses of the response of the Israelites. What did He say the people were doing?

15. _____

Turn one book over to *Deuteronomy Chapter 1*. It is now almost 40 years later, and the next generation of Israelites is about to enter the Promised Land. For the first few chapters of *Deuteronomy*, Moses retold all that happened during their time of wandering. Read *verses 26-27*, in which he detailed the incident with the spies. What did Moses say was the Israelites' response? And what did they believe about God?

16. _____

_____

_____

Although Moses had doubted whether he was the right choice to go to Egypt, there was a clear difference between how he and the Israelites viewed God. Moses had doubts but followed through anyway. We see that the Israelites were unwilling to go and they even thought that God hated them.

As a result, God was ready to replace them as His chosen people (see *Numbers 14:12*). The next "but" is in *Numbers 14:13-19*. How did Moses appeal to God here?

17. _____

_____

Notice Moses didn't say, "God, give them another chance. Sometimes they just get a little tired and impatient. But look at the good things they've done!" Moses agreed with God at this moment (remember, they were trying to replace Moses himself!). His plea was not based on the people's goodness or potential. Instead, he appealed based on God's attributes of justice, love, and forgiveness.

NEVERTHELESS THE PEOPLE WHO LIVE IN THE LAND ARE STRONG

Read *Numbers 14:20-24* and *14:30-34*. There are two "buts" in *verses 24* and *32* that show us a contrast in God's dealings. What was Gods' response?

18. _____

_____

_____

What were the reasons for God's commendation of Caleb in *verse 24?*

19. _____

_____

God forgave the sin of the Israelites, which means they were restored to a right relationship. However, their disobedience had physical consequences. With the exception of Caleb and Joshua, all the adult Israelites would die in the wilderness and never see the Promised Land. God would still fulfill His promise, but it would be delayed for almost four decades.

CONCLUSION AND APPLICATION

Caleb and Joshua's story is similar to Moses' — God directed them to go up against enemies that were stronger than they were. But He gave them assurances that He would be the One to accomplish victory.

- To Moses, He gave the promise of His character and presence.
- To the Israelites, He demonstrated His power through His past works, which He specifically commanded them to remember.

These stories can teach us a great deal about fear. When God called Moses to go back to Egypt, we saw that his initial reaction was one of fear. Despite the Lord's assurances, he was hesitant and supplied many what-ifs. What was Moses afraid of?

20. _____

_____

_____

When God called the Israelites to go into the Promised Land, what were the Israelites afraid of?

21. _____

_____

_____

NEVERTHELESS THE PEOPLE WHO LIVE IN THE LAND ARE STRONG

Why weren't Joshua and Caleb afraid?

22. _____

_____

_____

The 10 spies and all the people seemed to be motivated by multiple concerns: fear that they would die in the process of entering the Promised Land; lack of confidence in the promises of God; and forgetting how far the Lord had brought them already. In contrast to their fellow Israelites, Caleb and Joshua had complete confidence and faith in God to overcome the obstacles they faced. They didn't look at their own inadequacies, but toward God's power.

So how do we overcome fear in the midst of obstacles and difficulties? Let's look at a few passages in which the Lord teaches us how to deal with fear.

Turn to *Deuteronomy 7:17-19*. Forty years later, when the Israelites were about to enter the Promised Land, Moses summarized God's commands and Israel's history. Then he prepared them for what lay ahead. In *verse 17*, what did Moses say they might be tempted to do?

23. _____

_____

_____

What was Moses' exhortation to them in *verse 18?*

24. _____

_____

_____

You can also read *Deuteronomy 20:1-4* and *Psalm 105:5* on your own time. Now turn over to *Deuteronomy 31:6.* What did God promise the Israelites?

25. _____

_____

_____

God gave the Israelites two things to help them to trust Him:
- He gave them promises; and
- He told them to remember the things they had seen Him accomplish in the past.

He does the same for us today. He has given us many promises in His Word and He tells us to remember the works that He has already done.

There are many promises that God gives us so that we do not fear. Let's look at one. Turn to *John 14* and read *verse 27.* What is Jesus' promise for us here?

26. _____

_____

NEVERTHELESS THE PEOPLE WHO LIVE IN THE LAND ARE STRONG

Here are several other promises God gives us when we are in the midst of difficulty (for separate study if you have insufficient time in the group). He promises that:

- He will hear our prayers *(Psalm 34:17; 145:19)*;
- He will guide us by His Word and His Holy Spirit *(Psalm 119:9, 130; John 14:26; 16:13)*;
- He will always be with us *(Matthew 28:20; Hebrews 13:5)*;
- He will give us grace to help in time of need *(Hebrews 4:16)*;
- He will give peace when we make our requests known *(Philippians 4:6-9)*;
- He will work circumstances for us to grow into His character *(Romans 8:28-29)*;
- He will give us a way of escape from temptation so that we may be able to endure it *(1 Corinthians 10:13)*;
- Troubles are only temporary *(2 Corinthians 4:16-17)*.

For other promises specifically related to fear, you can also read *Psalm 118:6, Jeremiah 17:7-8, Matthew 6:25, 34,* and *Luke 12:22-34.*

Think about something that God has done in your life that you should remember when you face difficulty. Write it down here.

27. _____

_____

_____

_____

Now let's look at our response. First turn to *2 Timothy 1:7.* What characteristics are in opposition to fear?

28. _____

_____

First John 4:18 gives us a fundamental principle about overcoming fear. What is it?

29. _____

_____

In other words, focus on demonstrating love for God and others, and not on the circumstance that is leading to fear. Now, turn to *Philippians 4:6-9.* What are several of God's commands we can put on in place of being anxious *(verses 6, 8,* and *9)*?

30. _____

_____

NEVERTHELESS THE PEOPLE WHO LIVE IN THE LAND ARE STRONG

What is the result that God promises in *verse 7?*

31. _____

_____

_____

Now take your situation from the previous lesson. Is this a situation in which you may emotionally be afraid of the challenges, or the consequences, or the future? How do all these Scriptures apply to your responses in that situation?

32. _____

_____

_____

_____

_____

_____

_____

_____

What can you do to apply what you have learned?

33. _____

_____

_____

_____

_____

_____

_____

The Lord had set the Israelites free and promised them good land to inhabit. Even though they were up against a more powerful enemy, God had already demonstrated that He could accomplish the victory. Yet they chose to give in to their fear, losing sight of God's power to deliver. Fear led to their lack of trust. And as a result, fear resulted in that generation's never seeing the Promised Land, with the exception of Joshua and Caleb.

NEVERTHELESS THE PEOPLE WHO LIVE IN THE LAND ARE STRONG

In contrast, Caleb and Joshua are commended in the Bible as ones who kept their confidence in God's power to do what He promised. Neither Caleb nor Joshua conformed to the majority opinion, and they faced death by stoning as a result. Yet the Lord saved them and He blessed them with entering the Promised Land. May we be people like Caleb and Joshua, who overcome fear by placing complete trust in the Lord through obedience, no matter the cost or outcome.

Made in the USA
Middletown, DE
11 May 2025

75427116R00051